JOHN MILTON

Paradise Lost: Books I–II

THE CAMBRIDGE MILTON FOR
SCHOOLS AND COLLEGES

GENERAL EDITOR: J. B. BROADBENT

JOHN MILTON
Paradise Lost: Books I–II

Edited by
JOHN BROADBENT
University of East Anglia, Norwich

MILTON, his face set fair for Paradise,
And knowing that he and Paradise were lost
In separate desolation, bravely crossed
Into his second night and paid his price.
There towards the end he to the dark tower came
Set square in the gate, a mass of blackened stone
Crowned with vermilion fiends like streamers blown
From a great funnel filled with roaring flame.

Shut in his darkness, these he could not see,
But heard the steely clamour known too well
On Saturday night in every street in Hell.
Where, past the devilish din, could Paradise be?
A footstep more, and his unblinded eyes
Saw far and near the fields of Paradise.

EDWIN MUIR One foot in Eden 1956

Cambridge at the University Press

1972

Published by the Syndics of the Cambridge University Press
Bentley House, 200 Euston Road, London NW1 2DB
American Branch: 32 East 57th Street, New York, N.Y.10022

© Cambridge University Press 1972

Library of Congress Catalogue Card Number: 77-181884

ISBN: 0 521 08298 6

Printed in Great Britain
at the University Printing House, Cambridge
(Brooke Crutchley, University Printer)

Acknowledgements

Edwin Muir's *Milton*, from *Collected Poems 1921–1958* copyright © 1960 by Willa Muir, is reprinted by permission of Faber and Faber Ltd. and Oxford University Press, Inc.

The photograph on the cover shows part of William Blake's *Satan, Sin and Death* (*c.* 1808), reproduced with permission from the original in the Henry E. Huntington Library and Art Gallery, San Marino, California.

Contents

[There is no index. Authors and titles indicate excerpts.]

Preface to the Cambridge Milton

We have also considered him as a poet, and such he was, if ever human nature could boast it had produced one...in expounding him we have therefore always given, as well as we were enabled, a poetic sense...for a poem, such a one as this especially, is not to be read, and construed, as an Act of Parliament, or a mathematical dissertation: the things of the spirit are spiritually discerned.

JONATHAN RICHARDSON father and son *Explanatory notes and remarks on Paradise Lost* 1734

This volume is part of the Cambridge Milton series. It can be used independently but we assume that you refer as appropriate to two other volumes in particular:

John Milton: introductions. A collaborative volume listed under the general editor's name. For Milton's life, times, ideas; music, visual arts, science, the Bible in relation to his poetry; a long essay on *Milton in literary history* and *General introduction to the early poems*. (Each early poem will also have a specific introduction in its own volume.)

Paradise Lost: introduction. J. B. Broadbent. General introduction to the poem as a whole with chapters on myth and ritual; epic; history of publication; ideology; structures; allusion; language; syntax; rhetoric; minor components of epic; similes; rhythm; style. This volume also contains a full list of resources (books, art, music etc.); a chronology of the Bible and biblical writings, epics, and other versions of the material of *PL* (this section constitutes a list of materials for projects); and a table of the contents of *PL* with cross-references.

Paradise regained and *Samson agonistes*: their volumes will have self-contained introductions.

Examining, teaching, study

Milton's poems need more annotation to achieve a given degree of comprehension and pleasure than most others. Shakespeare, Donne, Blake, Yeats all demand annotation; but they arouse interest more immediately than Milton does, and so motivate study. This difficulty does not lie in the idleness of the reader or his ignorance: it was felt by Dr Johnson (admittedly a slothful man, but also a learned one and himself an editor). *PL* was one of the first English poems to be annotated. In 1695, twenty-one years after Milton died, Patrick Hume published his *Annotations... Wherein the Texts of Sacred Writ Relating to the Poem, are Quoted; The Parallel Places and Imitations of the Most Excellent Homer and Virgil, Cited and Compared; All the Obscure Parts Render'd in Phrases More Familiar; The Old and Obsolete Words, with Their Originals, Explain'd and Made Easie...* As editors we are all guilty, like Hume, of answering the wrong questions. As examiners, we're guilty of asking them. Milton's poetry is worth using in education because it is difficult; but we have to attend to the right kind of difficulty. In *PL* the serious difficulties are not the surface obscurities of

> nor to which transform'd
> *Ammonian Jove*, or *Capitoline* was seen,
> Hee with *Olympias*, this with her who bore
> *Scipio* the highth of *Rome*.   IX 507

They are the grave issues of sin, death, 'all our woe', grace, the use of beauty and strength, 'conjugal love'. Those are also the interesting things. But they tend to get left out of editions, and exam papers, because they are more suitable for discussion than for notes and tests. It's the same with Milton's earlier poems. *Arcades* is a little masque he wrote for the Countess of Derby and her family. It has a song that ends

> Though Syrinx your Pan's mistress were,
> Yet Syrinx well might wait on her.
>   Such a rural queen
> All Arcadia hath not seen.

In 1969 one of the public examining boards in England asked for 'a brief explanatory note' on those lines. In a way, the answer is simple if indelicate: Pan tried to rape Syrinx so she jumped into a river and turned into a reed. But whatever does it mean in the context? Can the Countess of Derby have suffered such an adventure?

2

Editors are helpless. Verity quotes Tennyson on the preterite subjunctive but does not elucidate; neither, of recent editions, does the most academically distinguished, nor the most school-aimed. I suppose we should be discussing the relationship between goat-god and woman, river and music; that is really difficult.

The best elementary exam on *PL* that I have seen was set in the summer of 1968 on *PL* IV and IX. It asked for either an essay, or a series of shorter answers on a printed passage: so two sorts of candidate were each given a decent chance to show their best. The essay topic was large yet crucial: in effect, did Adam and Eve *have* to fall? No nonsense about Satan's 'character' dragged in from the Shakespeare paper, or invitations to be romantic about Milton's soul. The printed passage was from Satan's soliloquy on arriving in Paradise, and the candidates were told so. Four questions directed the candidate to specific locales – 'What do the phraseology and form of these four lines tell you about Satan's own nature?' for instance. The fifth asked for the passage to be related to its parallel in Book IX. In short, the candidates' memory and attention were being helped; but they were being asked seriously difficult questions.

Here are some suggestions for overcoming the difficulties of Milton's poetry in spite of the editor:

Editing. Never learn footnotes. On the contrary, annotate parts of the text for yourself. You will find the answers to most problems in *Brewer's dictionary of phrase and fable* and the *Shorter Oxford English dictionary*; occasionally you may need a classical dictionary (such as Keats learned out of), and a handbook to English and European literature (e.g. the Penguin *Companions to literature*), and a concordance to the Bible.

Performance. Study Milton's poetry out loud to elicit its various-ness:

And cast the dark foundations deep	*Nativity* 123
Trip the pert fairies and the dapper elves	*Comus* 118
When that comes think not thou to find me slack	*PR* III 398

To study aloud means reading aloud to understand; alone and together; against music, chanting if you like. It includes acting the poetry. Don't try to act, say, the Muses and Old Camus in *Lycidas*; but express in a physical way (especially passively) some of the qualities or states of existence that occur in the poem: e.g.

look for the words applied to Lycidas's corpse (float, welter, hurled) and enact them.

Performance may include other kinds of manipulation. Consider how much we use other poetry – hymns, liturgy, pop songs, metaphors, riddles, ritualistic puns and fantasies. Extend the material from 'poetry' to include the sort of thing that Milton's poetry contains – language, mythology, theology, geography – and it becomes clear that we could *use* Milton's poetry in all sorts of ways, if we were not afraid. The advantage of great poetry is that you can criticize it: it stands up to you, and so gives you an idea, gradually, of what is durable and what disposable, or likely to rot. But another advantage of great poetry is that you can do many things with it. Other poets are not afraid to manipulate:

The sun and the moon shall be dark, and the stars shall withdraw their shining.   *Joel* ii 10

>   O dark, dark, dark, amid the blaze of noon,
>   Irrecoverably dark, total eclipse
>   Without all hope of day!   *Samson* 80

>   O dark dark dark. They all go into the dark,
>   The vacant interstellar spaces, the vacant into the vacant.
>   T. S. ELIOT *East Coker*

There Milton manipulates the Bible, Eliot manipulates Milton. We could probably enrich our own experience of the *Samson* passage better than this through music or paint – as Handel and Rembrandt did. Try representing in a non-verbal medium a sun which is as silent as an invisible moon.

Analysis. As you perform and manipulate the work, much of what it is about will emerge. Now start to analyse it more consciously. The best way to do this at first is on the fairly large scale of shape and structure.

What is the shape of this poem? Where are the soft pastoral parts, and where the strident military ones? If I shut my eyes and transform my image of the poem into colours, or music, a journey, a body, a life, what is it like? I notice in the middle of *Lycidas* a knot of darkness, clanging metal, infection, greed, blows. Can I refine my account, arrange it in terms of a single metaphor? What are those things doing in the poem anyway? How do they relate to the flatness at the very end, the spread-out hills, the distant sea, the set sun?

Then, what features in the poem set up structures of their own? This often happens with items that are repeated. The sun in

4

Lycidas recurs, along with other stars, with planets, with the moon, and with the concepts of the year, time, ripeness and so on; it seems to oppose the weltering waves.

Comprehension. Before interpreting *Lycidas*, though, we have to check our comprehension of its details: e.g. why does Phoebus in line 77 rank as part of the star structure? I put this late in the process because most of our small-scale difficulties will be solved as we perform and analyse the poetry. To put it in editorial terms, an inch of introduction is worth a yard of footnote.

Examiners have a fondness for those parts of Milton's work which (like the arguments in Pandemonium) have a paraphrasable content. Unfortunately, Milton is practically unparaphrasable, especially in such contexts. His language contains little in the way of metaphors to be unpacked. It is impregnable, for it works in large blocks of idiosyncratic syntax. Soon after you start to analyse the argument you find you have forgotten where it began. Milton's poetry does need a special kind of comprehension; but it is to be tested not by trying to 'translate' or 'construe' Milton; but by acquiring a sense of what you need to know. When you have grasped, by performance, and by structural analysis, what a poem or passage is about, look closely at the words which don't fit your understanding. In *Lycidas* you don't know where Mona, Bellerus, Namancos are. Look them up and you will find they are Anglesey, Land's End and so on. But these identities don't matter. What matters is, first, that Milton should have clad them in old names and mythology; and, second, that they are all western: they ring the sea where Lycidas drowned, and ring the sunset. In short, it is more important to register quality than learn genealogy.

How, though, can you recognize your need for knowledge in the case of an isolated word? Quite often, you can't. A lot of our ignorance has to *wait* to be informed, gradually, often accidentally. But you can avoid some traps by, again, attending to the verse and the structure, e.g.:

> Russet lawns and fallows grey   *L'allegro* 71

The colours enclose the landscape, so obviously they are important. Try to visualize the line and you will at once feel the need for help.

> Peace, brother, be not over-exquisite
> To cast the fashion of uncertain evils   *Comus* 359

5

As often in Shakespeare, you can't put any expression into the lines until you have found out what the words mean.

Attention

The reader of Milton must be always up on duty: he is surrounded with sense, it rises in every line, every word is to the purpose; there are no lazy intervals; all has been considered, and demands, and merits observation. Even in the best writers you sometimes find words and sentences which hang on so loosely you may blow 'em off; Milton's are all substance and weight. If this be called obscurity, let it be remembered that it is such an obscurity as is a compliment to the reader; not that vicious obscurity which proceeds from a muddled head.

Coleridge copied that into his commonplace book out of the *Explanatory notes on PL* of 1734 by Jonathan Richardson, the painter, and his son. Consider what the parallel in your ordinary life might be of the kind of attention you could give to Milton.

This edition of Milton

The texts are based on the latest editions published in his lifetime: i.e. chiefly *Poems of Mr John Milton, both English and Latin* (the earlier poems) 1645; and the second edition of *PL* 1674. But the text has no authority as such.

The spelling has been modernized (except where it would completely alter pronunciation, e.g. *anow* has been changed to *enow* but not to *enough*).

Stress marks (′) have been added where Milton seems to have intended a stress unusual for us, e.g. *óbscene*. Grave accents (ˋ) have been added to indicate voiced syllables in such cases as *blessèd* and in unfamiliar names, e.g. *Atè*. Milton distinguished between stressed and unstressed forms of *hee, he, their, thir*, etc. These have all been reduced to their normal modern forms.

Milton showed much elision of *e*'s, e.g. 'th'obscene dread of Moab's sons', 'th'heavens'. These have been omitted too because the elision comes more naturally if we read it with our usual neutral *e* sounds in such cases, than if we try to say *thóbscene* or *theavens*.

On the other hand, Milton's punctuation has been left almost untouched. It is not the same as ours, but you soon get used to it, and to tamper would alter the rhythm. In particular, modern

6

punctuation would interrupt the flow of ideas. For example, a passage about Eve's hair:

> She as a veil down to the slender waist
> Her unadornèd golden tresses wore
> Dishevelled, but in wanton ringlets waved
> As the vine curls her tendrils, which implied
> Subjection, but required with gentle sway,
> And by her yielded, by him best received,
> Yielded with coy submission, modest pride,
> And sweet reluctant amorous delay.   *PL* IV 304

Pause at each punctuation mark. Pause at all awkward line-changes, e.g. 'implied/Subjection' puts a pause equal to a whole stress between the lines. Let all neutral vowels stay neutral, e.g. *tendrils*, *required*, *yielded*. Run over unstressed words as in ordinary speech, e.g. 'She as a veil' is nearly elided as 'She's a veil'; but give all stressed syllables their full value. Don't be officious with the syntax: its sense is impressionistic rather than logical. The words implied–required–yielded–received are set in a pattern which represents a relationship, not a grammar: Eve's hair implies subjection; Adam requires that subjection of her, gently; she does actually yield – also perhaps gently; and he receives it, takes it back again – and then she goes on yielding it, her yielding and her reluctance to yield both an expression of love, her *delay* the rhyming answer to his *sway* (=power). It is not a sentence but a dance.

Milton's meanings are often etymological, e.g. *dishevelled* does not mean unkempt but let down without coiffure; *reluctant* does not mean unwilling but resistant; these meanings will emerge more easily if the words are dwelt on and given their full syllabic value – *dis-chevelled*, *re-luctant*. Reading Hopkins helps because he uses words etymologically. But do not elocute. Actors' voices have a particularly bad effect on Milton because his language is hardly ever beautiful or emotive – it is stiff and thoughtful, or colloquial and definite:

> The leaf was darkish, and had prickles on it,
> But in another country, as he said,
> Bore a bright golden flower, but not in this soil.
>   *Comus* 631

>   but all sat mute,
> Pondering the danger with deep thoughts; and each
> In other's countenance read his own dismay
> Astonished.   *PL* II 420

7

In the second passage there, one might emphasize the emotions of dismay and astonishment; but as a matter of fact, *astonished* means *dismayed*; and what matters is the shape, the structure of the lines; it is that, not expressiveness, which represents the fallen angels' bafflement. The structure runs: an angel – another angel – own dismay – more dismay. It is better to read with an eye to semantics than to histrionics; and to read as Milton did (with a provincial accent, rather harshly, with something of a sarcastic note, rolling his *r*'s) than with elegance.

The series will supersede A. W. Verity's Pitt Press edition of Milton's poetry published from Cambridge 1891 *et seq*. It is designed for use by the individual student, and the class, and the teacher, in schools and colleges, from about the beginning of the sixth form to the end of the first postgraduate year course in England. Introductions and notes aim to provide enough material for the reader to work on for himself, but nothing of a professionally academic kind. We hope that if any volume of text is prescribed for examination, some of its contents will not be set, but left for the student to explore at will.

In the face of the syllabus – heavy for many subjects – 'adventures of ideas' in wider fields, and the time-consuming operations of developing independence of thought...will be undertaken 'at risk'.

> Report of the Welsh Committee of the Schools Council, in Schools Council Working Paper 20, *Sixth form examining methods*, HMSO 1968.

This edition assumes that risk.

Introduction to Paradise Lost I–II

What is it about? Where am I in it? These are the difficulties of a big poem. One way of locating yourself, in time and space, is to draw a large-scale map of the kind of time and space, or people and places, you tend to meet in a lifetime, or a myth, or in literature generally. The two sketch-maps that follow are based on suggestions in Northrop Frye *Fables of identity: studies in poetic mythology* 1963. A good deal has been left blank in each case.

Time	Season	Lifetime	President		PL	Other literature
dawn	spring	birth	child? mother? midwife (=poet?)	VII	creation	
				XII	expulsion?	
				I	invocation?	
noon	summer	marriage	bride	IV	paradise	epithalamions pastoral?
evening	autumn	ageing, dying	villain?	I	hell	
night	winter	nonentity	ghost, witch	II	chaos	

Element	Positive	Negative
divine	God, angel	Satan, devil
human	equals together	tyranny, anarchy, isolation
animal	domesticated	monsters
vegetable	garden	forest
mineral	city, temple	rock, ruin
fluid	river of life	flood

You will notice that *PL* I–II occupies several places on these maps at the same time.

Here is another map, of the contents of I–II in terms of ideas or themes, with pointers to what the characters, places and events might mean, or what topics they might lead to in conversation:

Invocation	sin punished and redeemed Christian values versus the rest
Satan	the evil hero: heroic values versus Christian sin, punishment, revenge, despair
Hell and the devils in I	the problem of evil what to do with power, talent, technology
Hell and the devils in II	monstrosity: the false creation
Satan's voyage	quest, adventure
Chaos	the uncreated
Sin and Death	sexual anxiety

Introduction to Book I

1 1–26 *Invocation*

Argument. This first book proposes first in brief the whole subject, man's disobedience, and the loss thereupon of Paradise wherein he was placed; then touches the prime cause of his fall, the serpent, or rather Satan in the serpent, who revolting from God and drawing to his side many legions of angels was by the command of God driven out of Heaven with all his crew into the great deep. [Milton]

Epic ritual

An invocation is a way of starting a large public poem. It can be compared with other starting rituals. Here is the bidding prayer which opens the Anglican marriage service:

Dearly beloved, we are gathered together here in the sight of God, and in the face of this congregation, to join together this man and this woman in holy matrimony; which is an honourable estate, instituted of God in the time of man's innocency, signifying unto us the mystical union that is betwixt Christ and his Church; which holy estate Christ adorned and beautified with his presence, and first miracle that he wrought, in Cana of Galilee; and is commended of St Paul to be honourable among all men...

There the priest invokes the divine authority for marriage; he reminds us of its ancestry in Eden, and the relation between this wedding and all others, including the marriage at Cana when Jesus turned water into wine. The epic poet usually calls on a muse or goddess for inspiration; states the subject; asserts the ancient lineage of the hero; and relates his epic to previous ones:

HOMER *Iliad* trans. Lang, Leaf and Myers rev. ed. 1891
Sing, goddess, the wrath of Achilles, Peleus' son, the ruinous wrath that brought on the Achaians woes innumerable, and hurled down into Hades many strong souls of heroes, and gave their bodies to be a prey to dogs and all winged fowls; and so the counsel of Zeus wrought out its accomplishment from the day when first strife parted Atreides, king of men, and noble Achilles.
    Who then among the gods set the twain at strife and variance?...

> Arma virumque cano, Troiae qui primus ab oris
> Italiam fato profugus Laviniaque venit
> litora – multum ille et terris iactatus et alto
> vi superum, saevae memorem Iunonis ob iram,
> multa quoque et bello passus, dum conderet urbem
> inferretque deos Latio; genus unde Latinum
> Albanique patres atque altae moenia Romae.

'Of arms and of that man I sing...' Renaissance epics added love –

> Le donne, i cavalier, l'arme, gli amori,
> Le cortesie, l'audaci impreso io canto...
>
> Of ladies, cavaliers, of arms and love,
> Their courtesies, their bold exploits I sing...
> (ARIOSTO *Orlando furioso* 1532 trans. Huggins 1757)

– but they were just as patriotic as Virgil. Spenser opened the *Fairy Queen* by invoking Queen Elizabeth as

> goddess heavenly bright,
> Mirror of grace and majesty divine,
> Great lady of the greatest isle...

Milton's muse and his values

Milton obeys these conventions. He starts with an ablative, appeals to a muse, and asks her to 'say first what cause...' (28). Yet his invocation is different from its predecessors: for as it imitates, it condemns them; and it dedicates the poem not to nation, king or patron but to God. Instead of a hero's noble deeds, Milton's muse is to sing 'Of man's first disobedience'. Adam is not the founder of a nation but 'our general ancestor' (IV 659), 'our ancestor impure' (X 735). The muse Milton invokes here seems to be the voice of God which spoke to Moses, inspired the prophets and David on Zion (10), and was heard through Jesus. In Book VII Milton names her as Urania, the ninth classical muse, inspirer of astronomy. She had come to be regarded in Christendom as inspirer of sacred poetry and virtuous heroism. Even then:

> The meaning, not the name I call: for thou
> Nor of the Muses nine, nor on the top
> Of old Olympus dwell'st, but heavenly born,
> Before the hills appeared, or fountain flowed,
> Thou with eternal Wisdom didst converse,
> Wisdom thy sister, and with her didst play
> In presence of the Almighty Father.   VII 5

In Book I she is the inspirer of Moses when he wrote *Genesis*, and her mountain is not Olympus but Sinai. So Milton's muse is really God himself, as Logos or creating Word.

We can list the items in this invocation which embody the superiority of Christianity and *PL* over pagan antiquity and its epics:

disobedience	war, love, prowess
one greater man (Christ), the second Adam	man, 'the old Adam' as hero
heavenly muse (Urania, Logos)	Calliope, muse of epic poetry
Mt Horeb, Mt Sinai, Mt Zion	Mt Olympus, Mt Helicon, Mt Parnassus
Pool of Siloam where Jesus healed the blind man	Well of Aganippe on Mt Helicon which inspired poets

You can generalize the list into certain oppositions – childish *v* manly; divine *v* human. These stand for opposing values. You can also see that it holds to certain constants such as springs of water as symbol of inspiration, mountains as where gods dwell.

Mountains and waters

These mountains and waters form a set of symbols of how God reveals himself to men, as well as being a set of counters to the classics. Here are some details:

Horeb. A range in the Sinai peninsula or its border with Arabia.
Voice of God: here Yahweh told Moses to rescue the Israelites from Egypt saying 'I AM hath sent me unto you' (*Exodus* iii).
Vision of God in burning bush.
  Olympus where Zeus dwells.

Sinai. Site uncertain, in Horeb range.
Voice of God: here he gave Moses the law (*PL* XII 227).
Vision of God made Moses' face shine (*Exodus* xix).
  Olympus.

Zion. Site of temple in Jerusalem.
Voice of God: prophecy.
Vision of God: he dwelt in the ark in the temple.
Worship, sacrifice, priests.
    Classical temples; or Aonian Mt=Mt Helicon, part of Parnassus, where Muses live.

Siloah. Stream flowing from under Zion.
Voice of God: prophets spoke here ('oracle' in text): 'The waters
    of Shiloah that go softly' like the voice of God or the prophets
    (*Isaiah* viii 6).
Vision: it was also called the Pool of Siloam; that is where Jesus
    healed the blind man (*John* ix).
    Spring of Aganippe on Mt Helicon flowed with inspiring
       waters; the Muses drank from it; there was an altar to
       Zeus there.

Mountains and waters figure largely in *Lycidas* also. Yahweh was
originally a mountain god. See the mounts of heaven and paradise
(v 598 640, iv 131–235 543 825); and mounts of vision (xi 376,
PR iii 251).

Moses

An important set of parallels in the invocation has to do with
shepherds. It rests on typology, the system of similes whereby
things in the New Testament were thought to have their ante-
types, or to have been prefigured, in the Old. For example, Jonah
being vomited up by the whale was regarded as a type of Christ
rising from the tomb. That is why Jonah and the whale are at one
end of Michelangelo's Sistine Chapel ceiling; in one corner of the
ceiling is the brazen serpent that Moses put up in the wilderness
to cure the Israelites of snakebite; it was Jesus himself who
established this as an antetype of the crucifixion: 'As Moses lifted
up the serpent in the wilderness, even so must the son of man be
lifted up' (*John* iii). Here Milton calls Moses 'that first shepherd'.
It looks like an irritatingly obscure reference to the way that
Moses at one time earned his living; in typology it means 'he who
prefigured the Good Shepherd Christ', led Christ's people and
so on. So we get something like this:

Moses	*David*	*Christ*
shepherd, leader, saviour of his people	shepherd, king, saviour of his people	Good Shepherd, King of kings, Saviour of the world
supposed author of *Genesis* and the Pentateuch, partly about creation of the world	supposed author of the *Psalms*, partly in praise of God's creation	Word, Logos, Creator of the world
received God's law on Mt Sinai	planned temple for ark on Mt Zion	on Calvary abrogated law and temple

Holy Spirit

Milton claims a place for himself in the Moses–David–Christ
scale. At line 17 he invokes the Holy Spirit. His rhythms turn
liturgical; the invocation becomes a prayer; and he sets up this
pattern:

Holy Spirit

| impregnating the vast abyss | illuminating, inspiring Milton |
| creating the world | creating the poem |

or even this:

| *Holy Spirit* | *Milton* |
| mighty wings...dove | my...song...intends to soar |

The dove has many offices. As a real bird it is harbinger of peace
(e.g. at the flood *Genesis* viii, *PL* xi 852). As Holy Spirit it sanctifies
and gives authority at the baptism of Christ (*Luke* xx 1, *PR* 1 25,
71) and, most importantly for Milton, impregnates at annunciation (*Luke* i, *PR* 1 138; Donne's *Annunciation*; numerous pictures)
and at Pentecost inspires the apostles and gives them the gift of
tongues (*Acts* ii, *PL* xii 485). Some of these roles are put together
on a typological altarpiece at Klosterneuberg; one set of panels
shows:

Noah's ark with the dove
Holy Spirit at Pentecost
Moses on Sinai

So Milton's interest had traditional authority; but it was deeper
than that. All his invocations, and his other major poems, are
about how to dedicate genius and power.

1 27–330 *Satan*

Argument. Which action passed over, the poem hastes into the midst of
things, presenting Satan with his angels now fallen into hell, described
here not in the centre (for heaven and earth may be supposed as yet not
made, certainly not yet accursed) but in a place of utter darkness, fitliest
called chaos. Here Satan with his angels lying on the burning lake,
thunderstruck and astonished, after a certain space recovers, as from
confusion; calls up him who next in order and dignity lay by him; they
confer of their miserable fall.

Satan's heroism

Milton's assertion that Christendom is supreme helps with the
obvious problem of Satan. He is a hero but an evil one; similarly,

the *Aeneid*, say, is a great epic but a pagan one; the civilization of Greece in 400 BC was a great achievement but man-centred, not God-centred. As Michael says of another culture:

> studious they appear
> Of arts that polish life, inventors rare,
> Unmindful of their Maker, though his spirit
> Taught them, but they his gifts acknowledged none.   XI 605

To the Christian at any rate of the 17th century there was against this objection no appeal. The difference between a person, act or institution which, however imperfect, acknowledges God, and one that does not, is absolute.

As a matter of fact, the evil hero exists only in renaissance literature, between about 1550 and 1660. We know him as Faustus, Macbeth, Damville in *The aetheist's tragedy* by Tourneur. In a subordinate position he is Edmund in *Lear*. He may be almost everyday, and funny, like Jonson's Volpone; or a psychopath like Webster's heroes. He is often an historical king: Richard III, determined to be a villain, is an extreme case; but the audiences of 1600 were used to seeing evil, or at least weakness, in the divine casing of Richard II, Henry IV the usurper, John the murderer of little Arthur. We have had anti-heroes since *PL*, notably the Byronic hero of romantic verse; but the Byronic hero is more wicked than evil – his wickedness is isolated, not pervasive; and although heroic he is not majestic. It is the pervasion of evil, and marred majesty, that identify the renaissance villain–hero, and Satan. This, of course, is what starts us arguing about whether Satan is the hero of *PL*, and why he seems to have good qualities. We could clear the ground by asking the same questions about Richard III.

That will clear only a patch, though, because *PL* is not a history or tragedy but an epic. The hero of an epic had always been 'good'; indeed he represented the virtues of the civilization concerned – the piety of Aeneas the founder of Rome, for instance. He was not riding for a fall. There have been anti-epics, notably Cervantes' *Don Quixote*; but Don Quixote, the down-at-heels hallucinating relic of aristocracy, is obviously an anti-hero; Sancho Panzo his servant is an anti-squire; even his charger is a donkey. There is no question of Satan being like that, or Beelzebub. The first words between them – 'If thou beest he; but O how fallen!' (I 84) – these words echo the *Aeneid*, 1,700 years before *PL*. Its hero, Aeneas, talks of a vision he had of the ghost

16

of Hector, one of the heroes of the *Iliad*, the epic of perhaps 1,000 years before:

> in somnis, ecce, ante oculos maestissimus Hector
>
> .   .   .   .
> ei mihi, qualis erat! quantum mutatus ab illo
> Hectore, qui redit exuvias indutus Achilli   II 270
>
> In sleep, behold, before my eyes most wretched Hector
>
> .   .   .   .
> Ah me, what was this? how changed from that
> Hector who returns after winning the armour off Achilles

Yet although the allusion is to heroes, its effect is not entirely heroic: Hector was vanquished, he is now a ghost, and appears *raptatus bigis . . . aterque cruento | pulvere* (torn by the chariot and black with bloody dust). His defeat could be seen as Shakespeare saw it in *Troilus and Cressida* V, where Hector is butchered by a gang as he examines the booty he has won by killing a man in rich armour.

It is at this level that Satan's heroism is challenged or undermined. The details are not usually as obscure as the Aeneas–Hector reference; but you often have to grasp at a 17th-century valuation, or at least jolt out of your own valuation, for it to work. For instance, you may thrill to Satan's values (for it is all a question of values) when, as Satan reviews his troops,

> his heart
> Distends with pride, and hardening in his strength
> Glories

Or when at the end of that parade he cries:

> War then, war
> Open or understood must be resolved   661

What does that word *Glories*, at the end of a sentence but the beginning of a line, sound like, and do for Satan's character? What are the analogues in ordinary experience for 'War then, war . . .'?

We need to attend to two sets of deheroization. The first is rhythms in Satan's speeches, or in descriptions of him, which may sound grand but turn out to be hollow. Consider, for example:

> But I should ill become this throne, O peers,
> And this imperial sovereignty, adorned
> With splendour, armed with power, if aught proposed
> Of difficulty or danger could deter
> Me from attempting.   II 445

17

Is it pure lonely courage? What do the pronouns do here? the rhythms of the 3rd line? the alliteration? Secondly, attend to the values carried by the imagery and other associations that cluster round him, e.g. Hector, Achilles, whale, eastern potentate, tower ...They are often baffled, not plenipotent but only 'What permissive glory since his fall Was left him, or false glitter' (x 449). Most of Satan's heroic trappings occur in similes, where the verse drifts away from him into hazy areas, delusive like the mirage at II 636, or shuttered like the eclipse at I 594.

All this emphasizes what Satan denies (v 850), that he is a creature, not self-made. Here the final argument lies. We must admire Satan's vitality, and prefer it ultimately, as a symbol of a faculty for living, to Adam's passivity; but we can also see in Satan the possible corruptions of great energy – its tendency to pride, tyranny, destructiveness. These Hitlerian qualities arise from self-obsession, a fear of admitting to any weakness, to any power greater than its own.

Sympathy with Satan

Sometimes, however, his very disabilities, even his evil, invite us to sympathize with Satan. By definition, only the fallen can be what we call human (from the pre-fallen point of view it would have to be called subhuman: on this problem see William Golding's novel *The inheritors*). Satan does, therefore, more than anyone else in *PL* before Book IX, excite 'human interest'. He shows 'Signs of remorse...Tears such as angels weep, burst forth' (I 620; cf. IV 42 389, IX 463, *PR* III 215). He rallies the fallen angels, he dares the voyage through chaos; he commands his environment – he survives. We are bound, biologically, to admire his energy, resilience, courage, in spite of what mars them – indeed, because of what mars them; for we know only marred virtues; and even marred virtues may be better than none when it comes to surviving.

It is the vitality, however warped the life, of Satan that inspires the verse about him; or perhaps we should say that Milton's vitality was excited by Satan's plight, his need for 'dauntless courage, and considerate pride' (I 603), the extremity of the demand to see 'What reinforcement we may gain from hope, If not what resolution from despair' (I 190). This is part of what Blake meant when he said Milton was 'of the Devil's party without knowing it' (*Marriage of Heaven and Hell*). So far as Satan

18

represents the energy and intelligence that we should like to act with in such straits, we are all of his party. Yet the poem demands that we be on God's side.

There is no solution to this dilemma. I don't think there was meant to be. Presumably Milton did know, as well as Blake and us, that he was, as a human being, of the Devil's party, so far as that means valuing certain qualities. The long-term function of Satan in the poem is to test our values. What is good, and what evil? Where do we place dauntless courage and considerate pride relative to the virtues of the Sermon on the Mount? What is the place of heroism in a war being fought for a bad cause? Is there a point at which heroic virtue becomes megalomaniac vice? What do we feel about Satan's adventurousness compared with Adam's domestication? How does Satan's journey out of hell compare with Adam and Eve's out of Eden at the end?

You will have noticed that all Satan's human and perhaps admirable qualities arise as responses to his situation at the beginning of the poem – that is, defeat and punishment. This is probably the centre of the difficulty. So far as Satan seems human, he seems not totally evil; the malice attributed to him seems incredible; and then God's plan to destroy him, reasonable so long as Satan represents mere evil, becomes vindictive. So we get into a circle: so far as Satan is punished, he tends to become sympathetic, and God unsympathetic; yet without the punishment there would be no action.

The theological dilemma

It is really this dilemma that is at the root of arguments which purport to be about Satan's 'character', or God's dulness, or why God let Satan free, or why he let him sin in the first place; as well as many quibbles about whether hell is a place or a state of mind and so on.

The dilemma is more valuable than those arguments, though. It reveals – and Milton perhaps at some level knew it reveals – a weakness in the Christian development of the myths. Christianity assumes that God is totally good. It does not allow God to be responsible for the existence of evil; so it must have been invented by another – Satan. But why did God let him invent it? Because all God's creatures have free will. But Satan must be punished, and eventually destroyed. But punishment and destruction are acts which mar God's total goodness...To put it another way:

we need to project onto another the evil that puzzles us in the universe, or the misery or guilt in ourselves; but this other, when we call him Satan and put him into the Christian story, does not fit.

The poem, then, forces us to ask such questions as: Where does evil fit? How did Satan get into the myth? Is there a place for the concept of Satan anywhere? What else in the poem, or its myth, is contradictory? Are contradictions inherent in the inventions of man? Can there be a rational answer to the problem of evil – why did God let Satan rebel, tempt Eve, permit sin, misery, death? Milton's excuse for 'The high permission of all-ruling heaven' (1 212) is directed at the theory of *felix culpa*, the fortunate sin. Michael reiterates it when he shows Adam the future. Seeing God's plan for the redemption of the world through Christ, which Adam's sin has made necessary, Adam cries:

> O goodness infinite, goodness immense!
> That all this good of evil shall produce,
> And evil turn to good. XII 469

But Bishop Jeremy Taylor, chaplain to Archbishop Laud and Charles I, a man of straightforward piety, who died in the year *PL* was published, admitted that he could find no reason why 'God should permit evil for good ends, when he hates that evil, and can produce that good without evil' (*Doctor dubitantium* 1660). Milton's explanation in *De doctrina christiana* runs to about 10 pages and is unflinchingly unsatisfactory, e.g.:

There is indeed a proverb which says, that he who is able to forbid an action, and forbids it not, virtually commands it. This maxim is indeed binding on man, as a moral precept; but it is otherwise with regard to God.
  Ch. 8 'Of the providence of God, or of his general government of the universe'

Perhaps, then, we are asking the wrong sort of question: it may be that you cannot rationally join the words *God* and *permit* in this way? Theological arguments are always ultimately about the nature of the deity, that is, of the ideal of the arguing culture; expressions of feeling rather than elucidations:

Many there be that complain of divine providence for suffering Adam to transgress. Foolish tongues! when God gave him reason, he gave him freedom to choose, for reason is but choosing; he had been else a mere artificial Adam, such an Adam as he is in the motions [puppet plays]...
Wherefore did he create passions within us, pleasures round about us, but that these, rightly tempered, are the very ingredients of virtue?
Areopagitica

The possibility of sin is the ground of Milton's strenuous virtue.

Satan's psychology

I don't think it helps to talk about Satan much as a 'character': we don't have the evidence that builds up in a play or a novel. However, if we do talk about him in that way we should note that in spite of the rush of libido out to leadership and adventures, he suppresses a lot that wells up inside. He is taken aback by the love of Adam and Eve, but forces himself to hate them (IV 356); he is staggered by Eve's beauty but 'Fierce hate he recollects, and all his thoughts Of mischief, gratulating, thus excites' (XI 471); he shows signs of remorse but checks them:

> O then at last relent: is there no place
> Left for repentance, none for pardon left?
> None left but by submission; and that word
> *Disdain* forbids me...
> IV 75

He has to hold himself in tight for fear of disintegrating. He loathes himself too much to be able to love others (except other versions of himself such as Sin and Beelzebub). Theologically, he is hardening his heart, like Bunyan's Man in the Iron Cage. So he comes to despair, the completely God-less, completely other-less, condition, in which he will destroy anything he finds.

Even so, we shouldn't talk for long in this vein. As Sir Henry Harcourt-Reilly says in Eliot's *Cocktail party* (1949):

> Indeed, it is often the case that my patients
> Are only pieces of a total situation
> Which I have to explore. The single patient
> Who is ill by himself, is rather the exception.
> II

What is it in us (or Milton, or the 17th century) that needs the despair and the aggression of this Satan, and that needs to say that he is evil, or mad, or in some other way distinctly not-us? The imagery of hell itself is found in the dreams of schizophrenics: quicksands and fires, for example, standing for a feared engulfment; encrusting lava and hardening to stone as symbols of defence against engulfment (R. D. Laing *The divided self: an existential study of sanity and madness* 1959); but we know also that the schizophrenic personality is the product of human situations.

That is enough of morals and psychology. Satan is a figure in myth:

'And there was war in heaven: Michael and his angels fought against the dragon.' They cast down the dragon out of heaven into the earth, and he becomes Satan, and ceases entirely to be interesting. When the great figures of mythology are turned into rationalised or merely moral forces, then they lose interest. We are acutely bored by moral angels and moral devils.   D. H. LAWRENCE *Apocalypse* ch. 22 1932

The word *satan* means enemy, accuser, and tempter. Satan is therefore a personification of the forces that make for two kinds of evil in the world: as enemy he makes for external evil – discomfort, disease, death, the imperfections of life; as accuser and tempter he makes for internal evil, unhappiness, anxiety, sin. The Christian Satan is difficult to be coherent about because he is thought of as producing these two different sorts of evil; because the two have been linked on their own, apart from Satan (e.g. we think of *sin* as a cause of *death*); and because as a personification Satan has been mixed with other ideas. These include:

Fallen angel. Alphonse Didron pointed out in his *Christian iconography: or the history of Christian art in the Middle Ages* (trans. Margaret Stokes 2 vols. 1886) that though fallen the devils retain a degree of seniority in the cosmos:

The Iconography of Lucifer and the rebellious angels should follow that of the Hierarchy of Heaven. The origin of these images is traceable to the Hebrew Scriptures. Thus in Isaiah we read, 'How art thou fallen from heaven O Lucifer, son of the Morning! how art thou cut down to the ground, which didst weaken the nations! For thou hast said in thine heart, I will ascend into heaven, I will exalt my throne above the stars of God: I will sit upon the Mount of the Congregation.'

Satan was originally thought of as an angel, even when he came to tempt or accuse (cf. *Job*) because God was thought of as the source of all, evil as well as good. As God came to be thought of as the source only of good, it became necessary to transfer evil to another deity. So Satan became totally evil; but at the same time, as 'author of all ill', he rose in status, to be almost equal with God (in the Persian religion, Ahura-Mazda was a divided god, dark-and-light). But good must prevail; so we have the story of the angel Satan 'aspiring to set himself in glory above his peers...to have equalled the Most High' (I 38), being cast out of heaven into hell, becoming a devil (*diabolos*=accuser) and the malicious enemy of man. Most of this story is in the apocryphal books of *Enoch* and *The secrets of Enoch*, but Milton uses some texts in the canonical Bible such as *Isaiah* xiv.

Leader of devils. In the New Testament Satan is sometimes regarded as the leader of all evil forces, especially pagan idols (e.g. *Ephesians* vi 12 and *Revelation*); and as the ruler of this world whom Christ can save us from, and whom Christ will finally destroy (e.g. *I John* iii 8). Many of the difficulties of *PL* are really the difficulties of Christianity itself, in which abstract ideas such as Christ's redemption of the world, which operate in one 'language' so to speak, are associated with stories in a quite different language such as the serpent and the apple. This is particularly true of Satan. Not only was he probably formed by decomposing God (as above); but during the Dark Ages of Christendom he probably assimilated many characteristics of Roman and local pagan deities – e.g. his cloven hooves perhaps from Pan (or 500 years earlier from a Babylonian goat-god), his thunder from Thor or Odin.

Trickster. In many cultures, the activities of what we call the devil are attributed to *Trickster* (as he is called in folklore). Trickster has some sort of divine status; he is certainly powerful in the cosmos but may be at odds with his fellow-gods. He is dangerous, but often helps man. It is Trickster who shows man how to make fire, for instance.

Prometheus. Prometheus is the grander Greek version of Trickster. He created man out of clay and spittle.

Man, sacrificing a cow, tricked Zeus: he hid the flesh under the stomach, and the bones under the fat. Zeus chose the pile with the fat on top, so all he got was fat and bones while man kept the stomach and flesh. In revenge Zeus decreed that man would always eat his meat raw. So Prometheus, as usual quarrelling with the other gods, stole fire from heaven, put it in a thick fennel stalk, and gave it to man. Zeus punished him by chaining him to the Caucasus mountains and sending a vulture to peck out his liver once a day.

In that story, Prometheus is a god-on-man's-side. He sets up a little world of his own with man in it. Man's affairs don't much concern the great god Zeus except as a child might irritate a grandfather. The struggle is between the gods; it is the god who is punished. Like Satan, he is over-punished; but man retains the gift of fire, as in *PL* man retains the knowledge of good and evil.

In later versions, notably Shelley's play *Prometheus unbound*, Prometheus appears in another satanic role, the *rebel* against tyranny. This is a particularly awkward role for Milton's Satan because Cromwell had just, with Milton's approval, deposed Charles I. We are bound to feel sympathy for the righteous rebel, not only politically but also because he expresses our feelings of aggression against authority, especially when, as in *PL*, the authority is God – absolute, our father, and verbose.

Fantasy and Satan. We ought, though, to notice that Satan himself may be a father-figure in *PL*; at least, how do we distinguish between what is fatherly in the three commanding, potent males in the poem, God 'the eternal Father', 'the almighty Father'; Adam 'our first father' (IV 495); and Satan, whom Sin and Death call father in Book II? One of the curiosities of the situation is that only God has no wife; but all three have sons.

Also in terms of Freudian mythology, Satan may be seen as a projection of our anality. He is black, dirty, sulphurous, noisy (230 suggests breaking wind on a colossal scale). In Bosch's painted hell and in Dante's inferno the devil's anus is the centre. Luther reported that he was defaecating when Satan first visited him. But anality is itself a form of pre-genital sexuality; and we might regard Satan as a phallic fantasy in other respects, e.g. his serpent form.

Serpent. The serpent who tempted Eve was an animal spirit, like an Arabic jinn. Is this demon perhaps a totem, a creature chosen as badge or mascot of a particular group, to show where that group stands in relation to another group? We would assume, for instance, that as a totem the snake would be sharply distinguished from the calf (which the Israelites took in the wilderness; note that to have a totem means to worship it). This leads us to consider what position in the cosmos a snake might hold in relation to other things. Try fixing it by various co-ordinates, e.g.:

up/down	further down than man and other animals, much further down than birds and gods, for it lives in holes in the earth; yet also climbs trees?

24

wild/tame	not human, and not domesticated like a cow; yet not wild in quite the same way as a jaguar?
male/female	difficult to tell; or is it one long phallus?
mobile/immobile	difficult to tell; moves without visible means as if possessed with some instinctive force, or secret motive power.

The further you go with this kind of analysis the more likely you are to conclude that the snake is an ambiguous creature.

Dragon and leviathan. The Dragon of the Deep = the Babylonian monster Tiamat, ruler of darkness and Chaos, who fought against Marduk the god of light. This is the dragon of *Revelation* and the creature of *Isaiah* xxvii 'The Lord shall punish leviathan that crooked serpent'. So Satan = chaos. But chaos–dragon–leviathan came to be confused with real creatures, and their characteristics were applied back again to Satan. *Job* xli is a nature poem partly about crocodiles, e.g. their eyes shining underwater, 'Out of his mouth go burning lamps, and sparks of fire leap out'. That has been played back into dragons, and Satan, and actually into details of *PL*, e.g. at i 194, and in the simile of sailors wrecked on the whale–leviathan at i 200. In *NO* Satan is 'that old dragon underground'; and in *PL* x he turns into a dragon. In ii, monsters inhabit the wastes of hell, and Chaos is a person as well as a place.

Monsters are mixtures, compared with other creatures which are just themselves. Perhaps the change angel → devil → snake → dragon is not so very far: an angel is a cross between a man and a bird.

Satan and classical mythology

Most literatures contain versions of evil in the shape of huge monsters like dragon and whale. Milton was also drawing on the classics, particularly

> whom the fables name of monstrous size,
> Titanian, or Earth-born, that warred on Jove,
> Briarios or Typhon   197

It will be as well to consider here the whole set of Greek cosmogonies as they apply to *PL*. Don't be put off by discrepancies. Make your own versions from Robert Graves *Greek myths* (rev. ed. 1960 Penguin) and, for excellent illustrations, John Pinsent *Myths and legends of ancient Greece* ill. Jan Parker (1969 Hamlyn) or Leon Garfield and Edward Blishen *The god beneath the sea* ill. Charles Keeping (1970 Longman).

The Greek creation myths, like the Hebrew, descended from Babylon. There are several versions. Usually, in the very beginning, are spaces, times and forces such as Chaos, Light, Night. The 'Pelasgian' version is notable for *PL* (e.g. x 581): Eurynome, goddess of all, rose from chaos, danced on the waves in the wind. She rubbed the north wind till it turned into the serpent Ophion. He coupled with her. She turned into a dove brooding on the waves and laid the world egg. Ophion coiled about it till it hatched: out of it came everything that is.

The 'Olympian' version produces manlike gods: Mother Earth rose from chaos and bore a son, Sky, in her sleep. Sky rained into her pudenda and she then gave birth to animals and vegetation, seas and rivers.

There are three generations of these anthropomorphic gods and goddesses. Each set feared and dominated their children; each set castrated or deposed their parents, and then dominated their own children or siblings; and, although the rulers are manlike, in each generation there is an atavistic group (suggesting one of Satan's functions, perhaps – a carrier of primitive memory):

HEAVEN AND EARTH in the persons of Uranus and Ge
TITANS, GIANTS, MONSTERS ruled by the Titans, Cronos and Rhea
OLYMPIAN GODS ruled by Zeus

More details follow. The details don't matter but they are very interesting and should be studied first in the terms set out by E. R. Leach in his book *Lévi-Strauss* in the Modern Masters series 1970. The first thing is to notice the structure of events that run parallel in each generation. The next is to consider what they represent: is it successive waves of invaders of Greece, each bringing their own gods who displace the old? Or do the myths represent changes in the actual relationships between parents and children, as cultures changed? Or are they to be interpreted psychologically as intimations of what we all in fantasy feel about our parents and children? So far as Milton is concerned the important thing is that he had to admit these other myths of attacks on divine authorities by other divinities; and allow the greatness of Greek myth and literature; yet keep it all subordinate.

(1) Uranus threw the hundred-handed and the one-eyed into Tartarus. (2) Ge, indignant, incited the Titans to avenge their brothers. She produced iron, and gave a sickle to Cronos. With the sickle Cronos cut off his father Uranus' testicles and threw

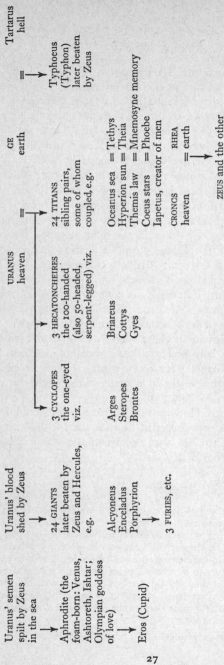

Tartarus
hell

Ge
earth

Uranus
heaven

= Typhoeus
(Typhon)
later beaten
by Zeus

24 TITANS
sibling pairs,
some of whom
coupled, e.g.

Oceanus sea = Tethys
Hyperion sun = Theia
Themis law = Mnemosyne memory
Coeus stars = Phoebe
Iapetus, creator of men

CRONOS
heaven
= RHEA
earth

→ ZEUS and the other
OLYMPIAN GODS, e.g.

3 HECATONCHEIRES
the 100-headed
(also 50-headed,
serpent-legged) viz.

Briareus
Cottys
Gyes

3 CYCLOPES
the one-eyed
viz.

Arges
Steropes
Brontes

Uranus' blood
shed by Zeus

24 GIANTS
later beaten by
Zeus and Hercules,
e.g.

Alcyoneus
Enceladus
Porphyrion

3 FURIES, etc.

Uranus' semen
spilt by Zeus
in the sea

Aphrodite (the
foam-born: Venus,
Ashtoreth, Ishtar;
Olympian goddess
of love)

Eros (Cupid)

Hera (Juno) childbirth, Ceres (Demeter) corn,
Hades (Dis, Pluto) underworld, Poseidon (Neptune) sea,
Apollo (Helios) sun, Ares (Mars) war,
Hermes (Mercury) messenger, Hephaestus (Mulciber) metalwork,
Artemis (Diana) moon

27

them into the sea. (From the blood sprang a number of new beings including the Giants and the Furies; from the semen sprang Aphrodite.) The Titans then deposed Uranus, and put Cronos on the throne in his place, and freed the hundred-handed and one-eyed; but (3) Cronos threw the one-eyed back into Tartarus. Cronos married his sister Rhea. He was warned that he would be deposed by one of his own children so he swallowed the first five. Rhea wanted to save one so when she was next pregnant she hid on Mt Ida in Crete. There she had a son, Zeus. Rhea gave Cronos a stone to swallow. Zeus was brought up safely in Crete. When grown up he made Cronos vomit up the stone and the other children. (4) He and these children now began a long struggle against Cronos and the other Titans. Zeus freed the one-eyed and the hundred-handed from Tartarus; they gave him thunder and lightning; with their help he won the fight, deposed his father Cronos, and (5) shut the Titans up in Tartarus to be guarded by the hundred-handed for ever. (6) Ge was impregnated by Tartarus and begot the monster Typhoeus or Typhon to carry on the struggle against Zeus, but (7) Zeus conquered him and buried him in Tartarus under Mt Etna. (8) The Giants (Gigantes: monsters with serpent legs) attacked Zeus with rocks and tree-trunks. He fought them in the Phlegraean fields of Sicily and conquered with the help of Hercules. Enceladus was shut down under Etna. The Giants were often confused with the Titans. At last Zeus held the world in control, along with the other 'Olympian' gods on Mt Olympus.

Zeus married Metis. He was warned that his son would depose him so when Metis was pregnant he took the foetus out of her womb and put it into his head; so when she was big enough Athene was born from Zeus' head.

I 331–669 *Fallen angels*

Argument. Satan awakens all his legions, who lay till then in the same manner confounded; they rise; their numbers, array of battle, their chief leaders named according to the idols known afterwards in Canaan and the countries adjoining. To these Satan directs his speech, comforts them with hope yet of regaining Heaven, but tells them lastly of a new world and new kind of creature to be created, according to an ancient prophecy or report in heaven (for that angels were long before this visible creation, was the opinion of many ancient Fathers*). To find out the truth of this prophecy, and what to determine thereon, he refers to a full council. What his associates thence attempt.

* Fathers: great theologians of the early Church.

The fallen angels, like the masses of a great civilization, are busy at technology and war, but they are compared to barbarian hordes, especially oriental and, via the crusades, they become the stuff of romance rather than actuality; and so they are denigrated – 'crew' (688), 'hasty multitude' (730), fairies at the end of Book I; and after II they play little part in the poem. They provide the standing army that an epic needs; and build Pandemonium; in II they explore hell, and in X welcome Satan back to it. But they have no effective function in the plot. Milton uses the fallen angels, and their ability to assume different forms, for certain purposes of his own: chiefly (a) to bring in history and allusion, often in similes, which thicken up the heroic air of I–II and extend the scope of the poem; (b) to attack idolatry. You can trace the swell of the similes from fallen leaves at 302 to the crusaders at 582 and back again to trees (612). Each idolatry has its region, its tribe, and in some cases its Jewish apostates, as follows. *Canaanite*: Moloch (Ammonites and Solomon); Chemosh or Baal-Peor (Moabites and Israel in Shittim); Baalim and Ashtaroth (Phoenicians and Solomon); Thammuz (Syrians and Jewish women); Dagon (Philistines and Ahaz). *Egyptian*: Osiris, Isis, Horus (and the calf in Horeb, Jeroboam). *Not local*: Belial (Sodomites); Mammon. *Greek*: Uranus and Ge; Cronos and Rhea; Zeus and Hera; Mulciber. *Roman*: Saturn. *NW Europe*: Azazel (banner).

Enemies of civilization

Within the general military atmosphere, the fallen angels are particularly associated with destroyers of culture – the pursuing Egyptians, locusts, barbarians. This theme is followed up with the ravages of Sin and Death in X; and especially the giants and other tyrants of XI: 'For in those days might only shall be admired; / And valour and heroic virtue called' (685). Barbarism was a real threat in the 17th century. The Roman empire was still the period of maximum order and culture for Europe. It had been destroyed by successive waves of barbarians – Germanic tribes who came from eastern Asia and displaced the Celts. They were pressing on the Roman empire throughout the 3rd century AD: especially the Goths along Rhine and Danube; some Goths even invaded Italy direct from the Black Sea. The Romans held them at bay, mainly by enlisting tribesmen in their armies; but in the long run that only trained the barbarians to fight better. In the 4th century, revolution in China extruded the Huns of Mongolia; they came west, crossed the Volga in 375 and attacked the Goths from behind. The Goths pressed harder against the Romans. 400 Alaric the Goth invades Italy; 400–9 Vandals cross the Danube and Rhine, invade Spain; 410 Alaric the Goth sacks Rome; 428 Vandals having crossed Straits of Gibraltar capture Carthage; 452 Attila the Hun invades Italy. For Milton there had been two major barbarian attacks since then: western Europe was nearly destroyed and forcibly de-christened by the Arabs who swept along North Africa, into Spain and across the Pyrenees into France until defeated by Charles Martel between Tours and Poitiers in 732; and by the Turks who besieged Vienna in 1529.

Parade of pagan gods

The most useful commentary on the parade of pagan gods is Milton's *Nativity ode* 173–228 where the gods slink away at the birth of Christ. There are plenty of details to follow up for their own sakes but to understand the parade itself, take a general view. What sort of error or idolatry is Milton getting at in any particular case? Of what truth is this a perversion? E.g. is Dagon, 'upward man and downward fish', perhaps a parody of, or even a crude effort towards, Christ's union of the divine and human? Another view can be taken from the question, What sins does Milton seem most interested in here?

Publicly, he is concerned especially with pagan polytheism. That the fallen angels had become the gods worshipped by pagans was orthodox doctrine; and in the 17th century they had also begun to merge with the fairies, pixies and goblins who were themselves the relics of native paganism (Milton metamorphoses them as such at the end of 1). Milton's attack on paganism is complicated on the surface but simple underneath for readers who were as familiar as his with the history of *Kings* and *Chronicles*. It is rooted in the Hebrews' monotheism: Yahweh was a jealous god, and total; he would not tolerate the more specific and therefore minor deities of surrounding tribes – gods and goddesses of sky, earth, water, corn and wine, love and death. He was angry when the Israelites took over neighbouring religions – the golden calf under Aaron (*Exodus* xxxii), Solomon's Moloch-worship (*I Kings* xi), Assyrian idolatry under Ahaz in the 8th century BC when Judah began to fall under Assyrian power (*II Kings* xvi). Jehu staged a reformation in *II Kings* x, and the last period of idolatry was reformed by Josiah (BC 640; *II Kings* xxii). Like many

Englishmen, Milton regarded the Reformation of the 16th century, and the Commonwealth of 1649–60, as parallels to Josiah's: they put down Roman Catholic and then Anglican idolatry; and asserted independence of Rome. Praying to the Virgin Mary, for example, was thought idolatrous; priests' vestments were fleshly; the array of official saints and martyrs seemed to endanger monotheism, especially when 'graven images' of them were put in churches; through the priesthood, and such powers as Henrietta-Maria, Charles I's Catholic queen, England was exposed to alien influence.

So Milton writes of 'gay religions full of pomp and gold' (I 372), and equates the Phoenician goddess Astarte with the Virgin by calling her 'Queen of heaven' (439). In a way, he was right; the Virgin, saints and martyrs fill a need for some object of worship more human than God, less pure than Christ, and female. Milton's own verse registers the need. He could dismiss many of the near-eastern deities as bestial because they took animal form – Astarte was sometimes a sacred cow, Dagon 'upward man and downward fish' like Caliban (I 462); the Egyptian Horus was hawk-headed. But when he says of Astarte:

> To whose bright image nightly by the moon
> Sidonian virgins paid their vows and songs   I 440

his soft rhythm admits the allure of the moon-goddess.

Astarte became, in any case, the Greek goddess of love, Aphrodite; and the Greek deities posed a special difficulty. The Hebrews had struggled against the polytheisms of Egypt, Palestine, Phoenicia, Assyria, Babylon; in the same way, the early Christians had been faced with the Graeco-Roman pantheon; yet Zeus and Poseidon, Mars and Venus, had been the subject of great literature. Its greatness was acknowledged more and more as Christendom moved away from it into the renaissance. These were false gods, yet beautiful, sometimes noble. In the *Nativity ode*, when they are exiled by the birth of Christ, 'The nymphs in twilight shade of tangled thickets mourn' (188). In *PL* the fall of Mulciber evokes delicious lines. It is impossible to think of Jove 'on the snowy top of cold Olympus' (I 515) in the same terms as the animal deities who

> With monstrous shapes and sorceries abused
> Fanatic Egypt and her priests, to seek
> Their wandering gods disguised in brutish forms
> Rather than human.   478

Perhaps this difficulty is more Victorian than 17th-century. Milton was ruthless: in those lines he admits that the classical gods were superior because anthropomorphic – there is a scale even in idolatry; but they were idols, only unenlightened gropings for the true God. Everywhere he imitates the writers who believed in them; but he unshakenly believed in the superiority of Christianity, both as a religion and as ground for liberty and love. In the end that superiority counts for more than classical art. In *PR* Christ rejects all Greek culture:

> Their gods ridiculous, and themselves past shame.
> Remove their swelling epithets thick laid
> As varnish on a harlot's cheek, the rest
> Thin sown with aught of profit or delight.   IV 342

The final irony is that the parade itself was a classical convention of epic: Milton's pagan gods are the equivalent of Homer's warriors marshalling their ships against Troy.

Solomon. You will notice how for all the middle-eastern religions Milton includes a case of Jewish apostasy. In most cases it is sexual; and in the cases of Moloch and Ashtoreth it is led by Solomon. He was persuaded by his foreign wives and concubines to worship alien gods; and so became a 'type' of Adam, who was also wise, yet persuaded by a woman to sin. This theme was of more than traditional interest to Milton. When he reverts to it for a short simile for Eden just before the temptation of Eve he echoes the alluring rhythms of the idolatries and romances of the parade of fallen angels in 1:

> Or that [garden], not mystic, where the sapient king
> Held dalliance with his fair Egyptian spouse.   IX 442

In England a public examination once asked candidates to construe those lines. What they truly invite is a series of more complex questions: why did Milton, or why do we, think of idolatry so much as sensual, and not just blasphemous, or just alien? What does it mean to be uxorious? Is it possible to worship a woman? Why are there no goddesses in protestantism?

Thammuz. Ishtar (Ashtoreth) and Thammuz (Tammuz)=Venus (Aphrodite) and Adonis (Thammuz the Babylonian god was called *adonai*=lord in Canaan, hence Adonis in Greece). See the items under Adonis in *Brewer's dictionary of phrase and fable* and Frazer *The golden bough* (use abridged ed.); Shakespeare *Venus and Adonis*; Spenser *Fairy Queen* III vi; many renaissance paintings. What makes the myth of the lord of life, gored to death, and mourned by the goddess of love, so important? Cf. the mourning of Jesus by Mary, and pictures and sculptures of the *pietà*. See a classical dictionary or Graves *Greek myths* for Adonis' incestuous birth from the myrtle tree; his connection with Persephone; and the anemone flower. Milton was very taken with the myth: cf. IX 441, and the epilogue to *Comus*:

> Where young Adonis oft reposes,
> Waxing well of his deep wound
> In slumber soft, and on the ground
> Sadly sits the Assyrian queen.

On this see Broadbent *Milton: Comus and Samson agonistes* 1961.

Osiris. Egyptian materials are difficult to grasp. Start from the *Larousse encyclopaedia of mythology* (good illustrations); visit a large museum and concentrate on the small objects. Milton's interest seems to have been partly in the notion of dismemberment: compare I 480 with the passages about joints and limbs at I 423, VI 344, VIII 620; there is another in *Areopagitica*.

Hell

We can't locate hell in certain lines: it is largely internal, especially in Satan (e.g. IV 75 'my self am hell'); yet the devils explore it in II. Milton starts us thinking about it when he explains *gehenna* in the parade. It needs explaining because in western Europe we have used the word *hell* (*enfer* etc.) to translate two Biblical words, Hebrew *sheol* and Greek *gehenna*. Both mean grave, or abode of the dead; but, like Greek and Roman *hades*, they did not necessarily involve misery or punishment. *Gehenna* did stand for an evil place and for destruction, but only metaphorically for a cosmic one: it was the Greek version of a Hebrew and Aramaic name for the valley of Hinnom, a gorge in Jerusalem which included a wadi called Tophet. It was originally a garden, then used as a grove for Moloch-worship, then desecrated and burnt by the reforming

33

king Josiah, then used as a rubbish-dump; hence always stench, smoke, flies. Other sources were also metaphorical:

Authorized (King James) Version 1611   *New English Bible* 1970

Psalm xviii 4–5

The sorrows of death compassed me, and the floods of ungodly men made me afraid. The sorrows of hell compassed me about: the snares of death prevented me.

When the bonds of death held me fast, destructive torrents overtook me, the bonds of Sheol tightened round me, the snares of death were set to catch me.

Psalm cxxxix 7–10

Whither shall I go from thy spirit? or whither shall I flee from thy presence? If I ascend into heaven, thou art there: if I make my bed in hell, behold, thou art there. If I take the wings of the morning, and dwell in the uttermost parts of the sea; even there shall thy hand lead me, and thy right hand shall hold me.

Where can I escape from thy spirit? Where can I flee from thy presence? If I climb up to heaven, thou art there; if I make my bed in Sheol, again I find thee; if I take my flight to the frontiers of the morning or dwell at the limit of the western sea, even there thy hand will meet me and thy right hand will hold me fast.

See also *Psalm* lxxxviii which is entirely about *sheol* as death, oblivion, the abyss, both literally and as a metaphor for weakness and grief. The NEB translation is particularly good.

Milton explains *gehenna* in the catalogue of fallen angels where he refers to Solomon's idolatry of Moloch:

> and made his grove
> The pleasant valley of Hinnom, Tophet thence
> And black Gehenna called, the type of hell.   I 403

Here is *II Chronicles* on King Ahaz (*c.* 730 BC), 250 years after Solomon:

Ahaz was twenty years old when he came to the throne [of Judah], and he reigned in Jerusalem for sixteen years. He did not do what was right in the eyes of the LORD like his forefather David, but followed in the footsteps of the kings of Israel, and cast metal images for the Baalim. He also burnt sacrifices in the Valley of Ben-hinnom; he even burnt his sons in the fire according to the abominable practice of the nations whom the LORD had dispossessed in favour of the Israelites. He slaughtered and burnt sacrifices at the hill-shrines and on the hill-tops and under every spreading tree.   xxviii

II Kings xxiii, about Josiah's reformation, is the classic passage on idolatry (and hence on the catalogue of fallen angels); it describes

34

how Josiah desecrated the valley of Hinnom and so turned it into 'hell':

He [King Josiah of Judah *c*. 620 BC] suppressed the heathen priests whom the kings of Judah had appointed to burn sacrifices at the hill-shrines in the cities of Judah and in the neighbourhood of Jerusalem, as well as those who burnt sacrifices to Baal, to the sun and moon and planets and all the host of heaven. He took the symbol of Asherah [a phallic timber associated with the worship of Ashtoreth] from the house of the LORD to the gorge of the Kidron outside Jerusalem, burnt it there and pounded it to dust, which was then scattered over the common burial-ground. He also pulled down the houses of the male prostitutes attached to the house of the LORD, where the women wove vestments in honour of Asherah.

He brought in all the priests from the cities of Judah and desecrated the hill-shrines where they had burnt sacrifices, from Geba to Beersheba, and dismantled the hill-shrines of the demons [satyrs]...He desecrated Topheth in the Valley of Ben-hinnom, so that no one might make his son or daughter pass through the fire in honour of Moloch...he burnt the chariots of the sun. He pulled down the altars made by the kings of Judah on the roof by the upper chamber of Ahaz and the altars made by Manasseh in the two courts of the house of the LORD; he pounded them to dust and threw it into the gorge of Kidron. Also, on the east of Jerusalem, to the south of the Mount of Olives, the king desecrated the hill-shrines which Solomon the king of Israel had built for Ashtoreth [=Astarte= Aphrodite=Venus] the loathsome goddess of the Sidonians [Tyre and Sidon=Phoenicia=Lebanon; modern Beirut lies between the two cities], and for Kemosh the loathsome god of Moab, and for Milcom the abominable god of the Ammonites; he broke down the sacred pillars and cut down the sacred poles and filled the places where they had stood with human bones...He slaughtered on the altars all the priests of the hillshrines who were there, and he burnt human bones upon them. Then he went back to Jerusalem.

We can see what was lost in this reformation – a religion full of sexuality, close to nature, and rich with art. Was there any gain? If we were to conduct a reformation now, what are the representative idols that would be destroyed?

It is really only in the more fanatical parts of the New Testament (and apocrypha and pseudepigrapha) that *sheol–hades* is used as a place of deliberate torture: *II Peter* ii 4, *Revelation* xiv 10.

At this stage we might consider the characteristics of hell in general, as we understand it, together with the characteristics of death, in parallel; e.g. *hell* deep dark fire chains gates...*death* buried dark? burnt?...Another way of looking at hell and the grave is geometrically: men live in middle earth, middle between the above and the below. The above is where gods live; the below is where dead people 'live' – or are they another sort of gods? In

Christianity, of course, some dead people 'live' in the above. Then we might start a set of parallels for hell and heaven.

1 670–798 *Pandemonium*

Argument. Pandemonium the palace of Satan rises, suddenly built out of the deep. The infernal peers there sit in council.

Mock-heroic

Voltaire thought the episode belonged to *mock*-heroic:

FRANÇOIS-MARIE AROUET DE VOLTAIRE from *An essay upon the epic poetry of the European nations from Homer to Milton* 1727

The poet seems to delight in building his Pandaemonium in Doric order with frieze and cornice, and a roof of gold. Such a contrivance favours more of the wild fancy of our Father Le Moine [a French artist] than of the serious spirit of Milton. But when afterwards the devils turn dwarfs to fill their places in the house, as if it was impracticable to build a room large enough to contain them in their natural size, it is an idle story which would match the most extravagant tales. And to crown all, Satan and the chief lords preserving their own monstrous forms, while the rabble of the devils shrink into pigmies, heightens the ridicule of the whole contrivance to an unexpressible degree. Methinks the true criterion for discerning what is really ridiculous in an epic poem is to examine if the same thing would not fit exactly the mock-heroic: then I dare say that nothing is so adapted to that ludicrous way of writing as the metamorphosis of the devils into dwarfs.

Other possible cases of the mock-heroic in *PL* are the Limbo of Fools III 489; cannon in heaven VI 568; metamorphosis of devils into snakes X 511. In *PL* the mockery seems always to refer to some genuine heroism; the question to ask of the later, 'pure' mock-heroic is, What is it actually mocking? See Dryden *Mack-flecknoe*, and Pope *Rape of the lock* and *Dunciad*; all imitate Milton's style.

Parody and metamorphosis

Of those other cases of mock-heroic in *PL*, one is about the technology of war, two about change. Mrs McCaffrey remarks that, in deliberate contrast to the peace of Eden, 'the denizens of Hell are obsessed with time and the heavy change of their condition' (*PL as myth*). As we have already noticed, they are obsessively busy; and they keep changing, either in metaphor or in the story (as Satan does too). In *PL* change is always bad: it is the principle of the fall, the antithesis of heaven; see I 84 313 424 462–3 598 779, III 634, IV 115 196 800 986, IX 187 1064, X 511 651.

36

The rising of Pandemonium is not only one of the devils' few feats; it is a case of change as well. The 'dark materials' of hell are metamorphosed into a palace, exactly as a 'transformation scene' used to appear in pantomime or masque; for it 'rises' like scenery, like an 'exhalation' (mist or backdrop, either). It is like the mirage of Rome that Satan tempts Christ with in *PR*:

> The imperial palace, compass huge, and high
> The structure, skill of noblest architects,
> With gilded battlements, conspicuous far,
> Turrets and terraces, and glittering spires.   IV 51

And it is a parody of how the heavens and earth rose out of chaos at God's command. It is the fallen angels' attempt to make a heaven of hell.

Behind the passage lie several sets of oppositions. For instance, what the devils build is a palace or city; Adam and Eve live in a bower in a garden. This is art versus nature, with art on the bad side. It reappears on the bad side with the gunpowder of IV 814, VI 482; and after the fall when Adam and Eve are taught the use of fire (X 1073) and Tubal Cain develops metallurgy (XI 560). Why should fire be hellish? Why should there be such a sense of guilt about technology *before* the industrial revolution?

The Pandemonium episode, like the whole of the debate in II, is also a parody of political man – 'expatiate and confer Their state affairs' (774). Politics is the technique of society: why should it be guilt-laden?

Mulciber

Lines 742–6 about Mulciber's fall are the centre of a controversy. Landor in his *Imaginary conversations* (1824–9) and Leavis in *Revaluation* (1936) objected that Milton lets such fluent beauty into the poem only to trample on it. Similar delicious lines, followed by rejection, will be found at I 446, *PR* II 350 and in the *Nativity ode*. It is a large and genuine issue for Milton. See the present editor's *Some graver subject* (1960) ch. 2 sect. 4. Meanwhile, we can see that the argument might go in either of two directions: (a) that Milton is not crushing real beauty but lamenting its corruption into sexiness or expertise; or (b) that he *is* puritanically afraid of beauty, sex, power, as we all are, and this is his expression of the fear for us.

Introduction to Book II

II 1–505 *Debate in Pandemonium*

Argument. The consultation begun, Satan debates whether another battle is to be hazarded for the recovery of heaven: some advise it, others dissuade. A third proposal is preferred, mentioned before by Satan, to search the truth of that prophecy or tradition in heaven concerning another world, and another kind of creature equal or not much inferior to themselves, about this time to be created. Their doubt who shall be sent on this difficult search: Satan their chief undertakes alone the voyage, is honoured and applauded.

The plottings and arguments of the rebellion in heaven, v 654–vi, should be read along with the debate. If you get lost in the debate, read it aloud with simple, even exaggerated characterization.

Defeated, and in misery, the fallen angels build themselves a palace and sit in it consulting how to spread hell further. This is how Milton came to see human politics; so the devils' debate is a satire on a privy council, a cabinet meeting and by implication a union executive, the mass meeting of a commune, a governing body – it depends what we want to satirize; or is the satire applicable only to one kind of meeting? See Orwell *Animal Farm* 1945.

Satan and leadership

Satan raises the peers' morale, establishes his authority and permits debate – or seems to: he has arranged for Beelzebub to put forward the plan he wants (379). At the end he takes on the 'hazard huge' of escaping from hell and spying out the new world. We must admire the energy of one who will 'tempt with wandering feet The dark unbottomed infinite abyss' (404). 'Energy is eternal delight' said Blake. He saw in Satan virtues which Christianity had denied. He used Satan as the hero of his own mythology, a rebel against repression; and when he wrote *The tiger* he picked up the rhythm of Satan's lines above to represent the cunning and dark splendour of natural life.

Milton admits that the fallen angels do not 'Lose all their virtue'; but the motives for their virtue turn out to be corrupt.

Satan deserves to be king, but of hell. What he could not be in heaven, he pretends to here. Milton punctures his pretensions: his throne is like an oriental despot's (2–4); the lines hiss at him – 'Satan exalted sat'; he leaves the council-chamber as 'Hell's dread emperor with pomp supreme And God-like imitated state' (510). Milton admired leadership, like Satan's, in Cromwell; but he saw little chance of its being pure. Satan is diminished by his own pride: 'with monarchal pride Conscious of highest worth' (428). In claiming kingship, Satan does what he had objected to in the Son of God:

> Who can in reason or in right assume
> Monarchy over such as live by right
> His equals?   v 791

Satan's first speech booms with hollow patches: 'More glorious and more dread than from no fall' (16) is designed to raise morale but it is nonsense. 'Surer to prosper than prosperity' (39) is the kind of proverb politicians use in their insincerest moments. And, like a politician, he flatters his subjects: 'Go therefore, mighty powers, Terror of Heaven, though fallen' (456). Can you rule without being pompous and insincere?

The other speakers represent the ways we react to any kind of hell. No-one votes with Moloch for war, or with Belial for submission; all vote with Mammon for 'peaceful counsels, and the settled state Of order' to 'Compose our present evils' (279); yet it is Satan's plan, put by Beelzebub, that commands assent: it allows them peace, yet promises revenge.

Peers of hell

The speakers in the debate are Moloch, Belial and Mammon, who marched in the parade of pagan gods in 1; and Beelzebub, to whom Satan first turned in 1. They are an odd mixture of political caricature; actual gods worshipped in Canaan before the Israelites arrived (as gods, information about them is scanty); and personified vice. For instance, Moloch obviously stands in the parade for idolized violence and cruelty, and in the debate for suicidal militarism; the others are more subtle.

Moloch. See 1 392, 11 44, vi 357, *NO* 205. The Ammonites worshipped him as a sun-god. Children were burnt in his metal idols (*II Kings* xxiii). In the debate he speaks as a bluff general. We stir to his last line, 'Which if not victory is yet revenge' but his aggression is turned against himself as well as others: he is content to deny the imperishability of his own angelic being; better be nothing than miserable (96).

Belial. See I 490, II 108, VI 620, *PR* II 149. He was not a god. The word *belial* is translated as 'wicked counsellor' at *Nahum* i 11 in AV and NEB; but Milton's connotations are assembled from 'the sons of Belial' in *Deuteronomy* xiii 13; *Judges* xix 22, xx 13; *I Samuel* ii 12; *I Kings* xxi 10 (all worth consulting). The phrase was a common political insult in the 17th century, used by both sides in the civil war. The Belial of *PL* I is lewd and violent, of *PR* dissolute and sensual. In the debate he is goodlooking, reasonable, suave. His style is economical, yet intimately stressed, conscious of the audience: 'and who knows (let this be good) whether our angry foe *can* give it, or will ever?' (151). He is intelligent. He sees that war is vain. He believes that God, being omniscient, will forestall guile (187) – and that God did not prevent it has puzzled all of us. He accepts God's justice: 'To suffer, as to do, Our strength is equal, nor the law unjust That so ordains' (199). Above all, he wants to stay alive and conscious: 'for who would lose, Though full of pain, this intellectual being ...?' (146). Milton damns his case as a counsel of 'ignoble ease, and peaceful sloth, not peace' (227). Why is he so contemptuous of him? What sort of sensuality, and sexuality, what sort of imagination, does he find in Belial to be so angry about?

Mammon. See I 678, II 228. Also not a god. The Aramaic word means wealth. 'Ye cannot serve God and mammon' *Matthew* vi. Hence it means the world as opposed to spirit. It was taken, like Belial, to be the name of a devil by mistake; was associated with Plutus, the Greek god of wealth; and so, by another mistake, and the association of gold with mining, associated with Pluto the god of the underworld. In the *Fairy Queen* II vii he is a miser in a deep cave:

> His iron coat all overgrown with rust
> Was underneath envelopèd with gold
> Whose glistering gloss, darkened with filthy dust,
> Well yet appearèd to have been of old
> A work of rich entail and curious mould,
> Woven with ántiques and wild imagery;
> And in his lap a mass of coin he told,
> And turnèd upsidown, to feed his eye
> And covetous desire with this huge treasury.

And round about him lay on every side
Great heaps of gold that never could be spent;
Of which some were rude ore, not purified
Of Mulciber's devouring element;
Some others were new driven and distent
Into great ingos, and to wedges square;
Some in round plate withouten monument;
But most were stamped and in their metal bare
The antique shapes of kings and kaisers strange and rare.

The whole episode is relevant to *PL*; yet money, or materialism, seems not to have figured in any *classical* hell. The Victorians used him as the tyrant of material greed e.g. in Tennyson's *Maud* and G. F. Watts' painting *Mammon*.

His speech is practical: they can't defeat God, they don't want to worship him; but they can make a heaven of hell by exploiting its resources and setting up committees. Mammon is not gross. He sees hell as a rich colony, and the fallen angels as competent survivors. He believes in good management. If we cannot refute his case we must accept technological bureaucracy, for the tenor of the poem is that we also live in hell.

Beelzebub. See I 81, II 299, v 670. Name = god or lord of the flies. A Canaanite fertility god, noted for being oracular (buzzing? cf. scene in Golding *Lord of the flies* where the pig's head speaks; and Sartre *Les mouches* 1943, especially Act III where flies = furies: the play is a version of Aeschylus' *Oresteia*). 'Prince of the devils', often used as another name for Satan himself.

The council applauds Mammon; but Beelzebub rebuts him with sarcasm: 'build up here a growing empire – doubtless!... to sit in darkness here Hatching vain empires' (314...377). Beelzebub's speech outlines the plot of the poem; but it also works as satire. The peers' applause for Mammon is likened to 'The sound of blustering winds' lingering in caves when the storm has passed (285). It is a vague, drifting simile, associating the devils with the hollow echo of a blown-out storm, with exhausted sailors and with their precarious vessel – 'whose bark by chance Or pinnace anchors...' It is the applause of a weary and defeated audience who cannot think constructively any longer. Beelzebub rescues them with his statesmanship, responsible, thoughtful, reliable: 'with grave Aspéct he rose, and in his rising seemed a pillar of state'. His very look changes the mood from 'hoarse cadence' to 'audience and attention still as night' (308). Then he proposes the destruction of the world – or the genocide of

Earth's inhabitants; or, if that fail, their seduction 'to our party'
(368).

II 506–628 *Occupation in hell*

Argument. The council thus ended, the rest betake them several ways and
to several employments, as their inclinations lead them, to entertain the
time till Satan return.

The council ends with 'trumpets' regal sound' and 'deafening
shout'; but the fallen angels falter:

> the rangèd powers
> Disband, and wandering, each his several way
> Pursues, as inclination or sad choice
> Leads him perplexed...   522

They busy themselves with athletics, war games, art, philosophy,
exploration, drugs (607–9). These passages have several functions.
The activities fulfil a convention of epic: in *Iliad* XXIII the Greeks
stage elaborate games after a funeral; in *Aeneid* V Aeneas holds
games on the anniversary of his father's death. But the style is
romantic ('airy knights'), archaic ('frore'), sometimes suave
Elizabethan like 'notes angelical to many a harp', sometimes from
early tragedy: 'Abhorrèd Styx the flood of deadly hate'. The
syntax is patterned in figures of rhetoric ('For eloquence the soul,
song charms the sense'), alliteration, catalogues, paradox. The
lines are rife with allegory, classical allusion, half-developed
similes of summer thunder. The devils' world, in short, is itself a
fantasy; so that too becomes a criticism of our world, of how we
try to calm our restless thoughts and entertain our irksome lives.
How valid is Milton's criticism? What are our versions of the
devils' activities?

II 564 *Stoicism*

The Stoics aimed at apathy, meaning non-feeling, impassivity,
insensitivity to suffering, disturbance and passion (the last word
does not mean emotions but being subject to them). They tried
to do this by a controlled acceptance of nature: 'Will what is'.
Cf. *PR* IV 300: 'The Stoic last in philosophic pride, by him called
virtue...contemning all wealth, pleasure, pain or torment, death
and life'. Pope *Essay on man* II 101: 'In lazy apathy let Stoics
boast Their virtue fixed: 'tis fixed as in a frost'. Stoicism was a
formidable alternative to Christianity; but, as Milton says (568–9),

its weakness is its strength: it is a philosophy of willed hardening. Milton offers Christian patience, which does not deny feeling, at IX 31. At *PR* IV 285 Christ rejects all secular philosophy. The best account to start with is in W. G. de Burgh *Legacy of the ancient world*; and:

JOHN MACMURRAY from *Reason and emotion* 1935
A morality based on principle, therefore, is a morality based on thought, on judgement, on laws governing conduct and determining intellectually what is right and what is wrong. Such a morality is based on *will*...The idea of will originated with the Stoics. It turns upon the idea of a struggle between reason and the passions. For the Stoics passion, impulse, desire – the emotions in the widest sense – were the source of evil. To live rightly was to dominate the emotional life by reason, and so to act by will; that is to say, in the way that you have rationally decided to act, whether you want to or not. Now that opposition between will and impulse has gone deeply into our European moral tradition. Stoicism was the dominating philosophy of Rome. It made Roman law. And the Roman tradition, which is by far the strongest element in European civilization, is a Stoic tradition. It lies at the root of our moral conscience, particularly as regards sex. The mediaeval idea of chastity, which went so far as to identify chastity with complete lifelong sexual abstinence, is pure Stoicism.

Torture and monsters

In this part of the poem the devils meet (as they don't in Book I) torture and monsters. Their particular torture is frustration. They are tortured with it again, and actually turned into monsters, at X 519. Can any moral sense be made of this? or is it that hell is a receptacle for what is horrible in us?

Anti-nature. To get at this subject, and the previous one, study one or two of the classical myths that Milton refers to, in depth. Then consider some of the actual components of hell. There are some continuities: e.g. the Gorgon turns to stone; sand and ice as materials of sterility. What sort of perversion of nature is Milton getting at? Is the concept worthwhile anyway?

Other themes. Book II contains a mixture of the practical (politics, exploration etc.) with the bizarre (monsters, chaos) which is characteristic of science fiction. There is a good deal of allusion to witchcraft: see Mary Douglas ed. *Witchcraft confessions and accusations* 1970.

11 629–870 *Sin and Death*

Argument. He passes on his journey to hell-gates, finds them shut, and who sat there to guard them, by whom at length they are opened, and discover to him the great gulf between hell and heaven...

The episode of Sin and Death is not Biblical. It is Milton's version of the epic hero's encounter with the guardians of the underworld. The most notable of these are Charon, the ferryman of Styx, and Cerberus the three-headed dog. Both probably derive from Egyptian rituals. The Egyptians ferried all corpses to the other side of the Nile from where they lived, for burial (see the model funeral boats in most large museums); they used dogs to guard the cemeteries; and their marshal of the dead, Anubis, was a jackal-headed god ('the dog Anubis' Milton calls him in *NO*).

The general idea of a sacred (or accursed) place being guarded by *monsters* was widespread – as in the snaky-haired Gorgons, the dragons of the Hesperides and the dragon which Beowulf attacked to gain a treasure. In particular, the snaky woman or witch is a dangerous but alluring guardian – Circe on her isle, the Sirens on their rocks who sang to Odysseus (and who were used to decorate tombs just as we use angels and cherubs), Lamia. Death too has been personified in other mythologies, though usually as king or queen *of* the dead – Anubis, Dis, Persephone.

The chief difference between these figures and Milton's is that Milton's are total ethical negatives. Persephone and Anubis were terrifying, but each was guardian as well as judge of the souls of the dead; and controlled the frightening forces of the ancestral dead, kept them from re-entering life. The myth often proposed a seasonal return of vigour (e.g. Persephone, Osiris). It seems to have been only in the middle ages that Death became personified as the diabolical skeleton of the Dance of Death, along with such other personifications as the Seven Deadly Sins (see Dürer, Bosch, Holbein, Bruegel). This again is due to Christianity's failure at times to include death as part of God's creation. In the same way, Milton's Sin had been personified before as a 'snaky sorceress' – Spenser's Error in the *Fairy Queen* I i 14 for instance. Her essentials are sexual allurement and sexual disgust. She represents a lust which embodies its own revulsion and punishment.

Sin tells how (747ff.) Satan conceived and bore her and then seduced her, his daughter; she bore Death and he raped her, his mother; she bore a pack of dogs which continually rape her, and at their birth she was deformed. You could say that this is an allegory of Satan's individual psychology: he leans on fantasy rather than reality; he creates anti-life. He conceives Sin as a figment of his imagination, then loves her as an emanation of his own mind; and the issue of that self-love is 'the meagre shadow' Death (x 264). In fact the allegory is drawn from *James* i:

Let no man say when he is tempted, I am tempted of God: for God cannot be tempted with evil, neither tempteth he any man; but every man is tempted, when he is drawn away of his own lust, and enticed. Then when lust hath conceived, it bringeth forth sin; and sin, when it is finished [full-grown], bringeth forth death.

The *relationship* between Satan, Sin and Death, however, is entirely Milton's invention. Within the poem, it is a parody of the Trinity. They use of themselves the language of God:

> Thyself in me thy perfect image viewing 764
>
> Son, thou in whom my glory I behold v 716

Sin is 'to reign At thy right hand voluptuous' (868) like the Son at the right hand of God. Similarly, when they build their bridge from hell through chaos to the world (1023 and x 282), Sin and Death pervert the creative act of the Son when he separated the world from chaos (VII 230). Satan, Sin and Death also constitute a model of the family in terms of its most fearful anxieties, as opposed to the model initiated by Adam and Eve (it's noticeable that *PL*, and Christian mythology, contain no complete family model):

Father/Satan. Actually a rebellious son of God the Father so stands for chaos instead of order. From his own point of view, father is always puzzled about whether he is not still a son. In this case he is also puzzled about whether he is not a woman, for he gives birth to his own daughter Sin, the perfect image of himself. In seducing her he fulfils the daughter's desire to be loved by her father but again upsets order. Physically he appears almost omnipotent.

Mother/Sin. Actually the father's daughter, so stands for promiscuity and incest instead of their denial. Physically attractive and disgusting at the same time. From the waist down she is snake – mysterious, poisonous, phallic (has she got a penis?). Puzzled about whether she is not still a daughter.

Son/Death. Actually the mother's lover so stands for a sterile *ronde* of incest – for death, in fact – instead of the continuance of the generations. Physically almost omnipotent yet invisible and formless.

Babies/dogs. Doubly incestuous, misbegotten; stand for sin and disease in the mother, instead of sacred maternity and fecundity.

But Sin and Death don't function consistently in *PL*. We are likely, therefore, to regard them as embodiments of concerns which have not been fully integrated into the poem, or perhaps not completely separated from the poet. Satan's 'conception' of Sin, for example, seems to express a characteristically puritan guilt about fantasy and masturbation as though they were evil. That is a fault in the art but it may be an advantage to the reader if it allows him to consider anxieties that normally stay unconscious. Obviously the central concern here is with sex as something that disgusts and frightens, and is liable to be punished by deformity or death. In detail, we have elements of the anxiety which boys used to feel (and probably still do about their mothers) as to how women's legs join on to their bodies; about the messiness of procreation, menstruation, birth; fantasies and guilt about incest, re-entering the womb and so on; confusions between the womb and the stomach; fear that sex kills, or that a man making love to a woman is killing her. Imagery relevant to these anxieties goes on all through the poem:

> Into this wild abyss,
> The womb of nature and perhaps her grave,
> Of neither sea, nor shore, nor air, nor fire,
> But all these in their pregnant causes mixed...   910

Compare the horrible imagery of their second appearance, in *PL* x, where they construct a permanent causeway from hell to the world: they hover on the waters of chaos like a hatching bird; Death coagulates the primeval slime 'with his mace petrific' (204), an anti-phallus. It is easy to make lists of these anxieties. The difficult thing is to genuinely admit that we share them too. Failure to embrace our anxieties as human is precisely Milton's failure: what he feared and hated in himself – lust, death – he projected onto monsters. It may be better to kiss the Loathly Lady.

46

Argument. ...with what difficulty he passes through, directed by Chaos, the power of the place, to the sight of this new world which he sought.

Chaos and Night, 'and the dreaded name Of Demogorgon', and Orcus and Ades, and the other members of the 'dark pavilion', do not reappear in *PL*. This is quite unlike the wovenness we expect of characters in a novel. In epic, however, figures may emerge in a single tableau because the structure is episodic – war, voyage, court, garden. As beings, Chaos and the others are pre-Olympian gods. To that extent they associate with all those 'whom the fables name of monstrous size, Titanian, or Earthborn, that warred on Jove...' (I 197). So far these beings have been used like that, in similes, and rather vaguely in the description of the outskirts of hell 'Where all life dies, death lives, and nature breeds Perverse, all monstrous, all prodigious things' (II 624). Now we meet them independently of hell or heaven, neither evil nor good, but amoral; very ancient; dark; anarchic. They are not just pre-Olympian, like the Titans, but pre-natural, 'ancestors of nature'; and, since nature is that which has been created, they are increate, 'without form and void' as *Genesis* puts it. So the visage of Chaos is literally 'incomposed', not put together (989).

These figures had family trees in some early cosmogonies; for example:

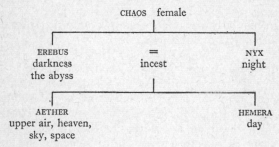

It is characteristic of these ancient cosmogonies that they start the universe with space-stuff and time-space. Chaos is a space but also the stuff the world will be made of (cf. an actual mother); Night, Day, Sky and so on are time-spaces; but at the next stage of the cosmogony the times are accurately divided by lights moving in those spaces. It is much later that we have the notion of a god shaping the space-stuff into things, ordering the times and so on. Milton of course believed in that kind of divine creation. He is careful with his views on the position of chaos as stuff in the divine plan. It is 'The womb of nature and *perhaps* her grave' (II 911: nobody knows what God will do with the world-stuff at the end of the world). It must go on being formless 'Unless the almighty Maker them ordain His dark materials to create new worlds'.

But of course the deeper function of this episode is to present us with these figures not as gods, or personifications of chaos or night, but as forces, powers of darkness, 'spirits of this nethermost abyss'. In that role they are internal. We can see their importance by beginning to elaborate their chief qualities:

Amoral. For the individual this suggests the time before speech, before obedience, the untrained time when all behaviour was acceptable for it consisted only in feeding and sleeping.

Ancient. Does this refer to our experience of the very old when we are very young? or to an interest in the question, What was there before time? or ancestral ghosts?

Dark. The normal adjective for what is guiltladen and secret. Is it to do with our own 'dark thoughts', or the places where we must not go, 'The secrets of the hoary deep', the womb?

Anarchic. Similarly may refer to our own unformed uterine state, or to the conflicts of our mind.

From there we can go on easily enough to chaos as a place. Again, it may be a condition of the mind; or the womb we so mysteriously came out of before for us time began, and to which we must not return; or the grave in the sense that we shall revert to a formless condition, and to timeless dark, at death.

But chaos is mainly a place of cosmological interest: the question, Where do babies come from? is on the cosmic scale the question, What was there before the universe? This is a question we should ask independently of *PL*, for the present. The answer seems to be either (a) Nothing; the question, that is, is meaningless; the universe began with an explosion (the big bang theory); or (b) The universe has always existed; it goes on becoming indefinitely (the continuous creation theory). Then we have to ask what the moral implications of the two theories are? Modern theories agree, though, in not bothering so much about the origins of matter as with the *way* in which the nuclear power, inherent in matter, generated worlds.

For Milton, as for most who had thought about it then, there had to be a reservoir of stuff for the universe to be shaped out of; chaos is that reservoir. Given the stuff, then, his interest focuses on the stuff's unshapedness, yet on its potential for the shapes we know. Milton (here at any rate) believed in atoms as the basis of matter. In this he followed the Roman philosopher Lucretius who in 55 BC wrote an epic about natural sciences. He

> saw the flaring atom-streams
> And torrents of her myriad universe,
> Ruining along the illimitable inane.
>
> TENNYSON *Lucretius*

But for Milton the atoms were not like our atoms, little planetary systems with their own charges of power; they were like little marbles. Only an external force could combine them. In some cosmogonies this force was a kind of magnetism; in others it was love; for Milton of course it was God's word. Until then, they jostle meaninglessly. It is this jostling which seems to interest Milton most. He applies a great deal of military imagery to it – war, siege and so on – especially of an internecine kind. This amounts to a symbolic statement: without God's intervention, the world, and people, are subject to a chaos of forces or passions or uncertainties; there is mere collision, civil war, the rule of chance or brute force: anarchy. The moral is political. Anarchy and civil war were the great political fears of the time, from Shakespeare's early history plays about the Wars of the Roses, to Hobbes's *Leviathan*, published after the actual civil war, in 1651. Hobbes was also an atomist; and he saw human beings in some original state of nature as like Milton's warring atoms, just fighting each other. Hobbes's remedy was absolute submission to the state's rule of law. Milton's was submission to God's law first, and prevailingly if it seemed to contradict the state's.

Clearly one function of the chaos fantasy is to remind us what we think the world is made of: a call to admit the nature of things, that is. Another function is to remind us what we think the qualities of those things are: a call to consider, and to order, *our experience of* things. Is 'nature' chaos, or creation?

Book I

O F MAN'S FIRST disobedience, and the fruit
Of that forbidden tree, whose mortal taste
Brought death into the world, and all our woe,
With loss of Eden, till one greater Man
Restore us, and regain the blissful seat,　　　　　　5
Sing heavenly Muse, that on the secret top
Of Oreb, or of Sinai, didst inspire
That shepherd who first taught the chosen seed
In the beginning how the heavens and earth
Rose out of chaos; or if Sion hill　　　　　　　10
Delight thee more, and Siloa's brook that flowed
Fast by the oracle of God: I thence
Invoke thy aid to my adventurous song,
That with no middle flight intends to soar
Above the Aónian mount, while it pursues　　　　15
Things unattempted yet in prose or rhyme.

1 **Of** usual for titles e.g. M's pamphlets. Latin *de*. **Man's...disobedience**
mankind's sin as opposed to the individual's heroism in other epics.
fruit apple, result.　　2 **tree** the forbidding is at IV 420. **mortal** deadly.
3 **world...all...woe** words of totality and lament; with the sound [ɔ]
in *mortal* they echo through *PL*, e.g. VIII 333, X 817, XI 283 632, XII 313.
4 **one greater Man** Jesus the 'second Adam' of *I Corinthians* XV.
That is in the far future; 'our woe' is present; the invocation's tenses
suggest *PL*'s location in time.　　5 **Restore** replace; redeem (theological
term). The sentence, still waiting for its verb, is linked by repetitions like
re- and [ɔ]. **seat** abode i.e. paradise.　　7 **Oreb...Sinai** holy mountains:
Moses saw God in a burning bush in Horeb; on Sinai he took down the
law from God *Exodus* iii xix, *PL* XII 227.　　9 **beginning** first words of
Genesis. Note beginning words here and in 1, 8 etc.; cf. *Four quartets*.
10 **Sion...Siloa** the muse may prefer to inspire him from Mt Zion where
the temple stood in Jerusalem; or from the stream that flowed below it
where prophets spoke (oracle), and Jesus gave a blind man sight *John* ix.
If she does prefer one of these, then he invokes her from that place.
14 **middle** the middle air was a cold damp layer up to 7 miles high; abode
of gods and devils I 515.　　16 **unattempted** usual epic boast; but the
17c did think poetry had not yet tackled Christian materials properly.

And chiefly thou O Spirit, that dost prefer
Before all temples the upright heart and pure,
Instruct me, for thou know'st; thou from the first
Wast present, and with mighty wings outspread   20
Dove-like sat'st brooding on the vast abyss
And mad'st it pregnant: what in me is dark
Illumine, what is low raise and support;
That to the highth of this great argument
I may assert eternal providence,   25
And justify the ways of God to men.

     Say first, for heaven hides nothing from thy view
Nor the deep tract of hell, say first what cause
Moved our grand parents in that happy state,
Favoured of heaven so highly, to fall off   30
From their Creator, and transgress his will
For one restraint, lords of the world besides?
Who first seduced them to that foul revolt?
The infernal serpent; he it was, whose guile
Stirred up with envy and revenge, deceived   35
The mother of mankind, what time his pride
Had cast him out from heaven, with all his host
Of rebel angels, by whose aid aspiring
To set himself in glory above his peers,

18 temples 'know ye not that your body is the temple of the Holy
Ghost?' *I Corinthians* vi. Asserts protestant preference for inward over
public sanctity; and gets from hills and streams to M's mind. Tone
liturgical.   **21 brooding** 'and the Spirit of God moved [hovered] upon
the face of the waters [abyss, chaos]' *Genesis* i.   **22 dark** M was blind
by 1652 and did not start *PL* seriously till *c.* 1655.   **24 highth** normal
usage. **argument** subject.   **25 eternal providence** God's beneficent
plan, the 'idea' that the divine mind has for the world, as distinguished
from his 'ways', his interventions in human affairs. **assert** vindicate.
26 justify a Latin sense is demonstrate. In the Bible it means prove right,
especially when God's grace gives righteousness to man e.g. *Romans* viii.
It is not worth arguing what M means exactly.   **28 Nor** neither heaven
nor even hell is hid from you, Muse or Spirit.   **29 grand** ultimate. Tone
grand too.   **30 fall off from** desert; political as well as theological
sense. [ɔ] sounds again.   **32 For one**... over the single prohibition
'not to taste that fruit, whoever tempted' x 13; apart from that they were
'lords of all' IV 290 430.   **39 peers** equals.

51

He trusted to have equalled the most High,   40
If he opposed; and with ambitious aim
Against the throne and monarchy of God
Raised impious war in heaven and battle proud
With vain attempt. Him the almighty Power
Hurled headlong flaming from the ethéreal sky   45
With hideous ruin and combustion down
To bottomless perdition, there to dwell
In adamantine chains and penal fire,
Who durst defy the Omnipotent to arms.
Nine times the space that measures day and night   50
To mortal men, he with his horrid crew
Lay vanquished, rolling in the fiery gulf
Confounded though immortal: but his doom
Reserved him to more wrath; for now the thought
Both of lost happiness and lasting pain   55
Torments him; round he throws his baleful eyes
That witnessed huge affliction and dismay
Mixed with obdurate pride and steadfast hate:
At once as far as angels' ken he views
The dismal situation waste and wild,   60
A dungeon horrible, on all sides round
As one great furnace flamed, yet from those flames
No light, but rather darkness visible
Served only to discover sights of woe,

40 trusted was confident. most High trans. Hebrew name for God,
Elohim. The titles M gives God and Satan, and they give each other, are
signs for attitudes: here it is serpent versus Elohim.   44 The first phrase
empties the heroism of the lines before. The story begins here, taking up
from VI 867. The tense is present at 56.   45 ethereal sky heaven.
46 ruin falling: Latin ruina. These lines incorporate the few Biblical texts
about Satan's fall, e.g. 'I will exalt my throne above the stars of God...I
will be like the most High' Isaiah xiv; 'I beheld Satan as lightning fall from
heaven' Luke x; cf. II Peter ii Jude Rev. xx. The syntactical frame him...
from...with...down...there...who may confuse but represents
stages of fall and binding?   48 adamant fabulous impregnable rock.
51 horrid crew atrocious troops – both words stronger then.   52 gulf
lake of fire, traditional feature of hell.   53 doom his sentence continued
with more to exasperate him.   56 baleful malicious, and woeful. His
eyes express (witnessed) affliction etc.   59 angels' ken the far sight of
angels.   61 horrible appalling.   64 discover reveal. Many words

Regions of sorrow, doleful shades, where peace 65
And rest can never dwell, hope never comes
That comes to all; but torture without end
Still urges, and a fiery deluge, fed
With ever-burning sulphur unconsumed:
Such place eternal Justice had prepared 70
For those rebellious, here their prison ordained
In utter darkness, and their portion set
As far removed from God and light of heaven
As from the centre thrice to the utmost pole.
O how unlike the place from whence they fell! 75
There the companions of his fall, o'erwhelmed
With floods and whirlwinds of tempestuous fire,
He soon discerns, and weltering by his side
One next himself in power, and next in crime,
Long after known in Palestine, and named 80
Beëlzebub. To whom the arch-enemy,
And thence in heaven called Satan, with bold words
Breaking the horrid silence thus began.

If thou beest he; but O how fallen! how changed
From him, who in the happy realms of light 85
Clothed with transcendent brightness didst outshine
Myriads though bright: if he whom mutual league,
United thoughts and counsels, equal hope
And hazard in the glorious enterprise,
Joined with me once, now misery hath joined 90

here keep etymological sense so are stronger than today, e.g. dismal, situation, doleful, confounded, infernal, perdition. **65 shades** dark and ghostly places. **69 sulphur** the brimstone of hell; and stench. **71 those rebellious** angels understood – a common compression here. **74 centre** of universe and earth; to pole of outermost sphere. **75** Line stands back for an objective pause. Assonance pole-fell-fall. **79** The second phrase kicks. **81 Beëlzebub** Satan's henchman. See introductions. **82 thence** because the word Satan means adversary. **83 thus began** first of a series of formal but usual ways of introducing speech in epic. **84** Speech falters; he's not sure it is B because they have so degenerated; so in 86 *didst* is wrong; in 87 *though* is short for 'however bright they were' and 'If he'='If thou be'st he' again. **90 Joined...joined** a kind of rhyme called epanalepsis; pron. jined.

In equal ruin: into what pit thou seest
From what highth fallen, so much the stronger proved
He with his thunder: and till then who knew
The force of those dire arms? Yet not for those
Nor what the potent Victor in his rage   95
Can else inflict do I repent or change,
Though changed in outward lustre, that fixed mind
And high disdain, from sense of injured merit,
That with the mightiest raised me to contend,
And to the fierce contention brought along   100
Innumerable force of spirits armed
That durst dislike his reign, and me preferring,
His utmost power with adverse power opposed
In dubious battle on the plains of heaven,
And shook his throne. What though the field be lost? 105
All is not lost; the unconquerable will,
And study of revenge, immortal hate,
And courage never to submit or yield:
And what is else not to be overcome?
That glory never shall his wrath or might   110
Extort from me. To bow and sue for grace
With suppliant knee, and deify his power
Who from the terror of this arm so late
Doubted his empire, that were low indeed,
That were an ignominy and shame beneath   115
This downfall; since by fate the strength of gods
And this empyreal substance cannot fail,
Since through experience of this great event

93 He curt pronoun for God.   98 injured merit he rebelled for jealousy
of the Son; see initial conspiracy with Beëlzebub v 670.   99 contend...
contention another rhyme effect, traductio. Bentley said 'Very dry this,
and jejune'.   103 Heavy stresses on ut- ad- -posed.   104 dubious
uncertain of result.   105 At least 3 stresses in first phrase. Churchill
quoted the next few lines.   109 And in what else does not being overcome consist?   114 Doubted there was no doubt: the Son was invincible.   115 Ignominy pron. ígnomy here.   116 fate at v 853 he
claims the angels (gods) were not created by God but self-begotten in the
process of fate; so they may be fated to win. Paganism.   117 empyreal
substance the heavenly matter, like flame (Gk. *pyr* = fire), that angels are
made of; infinitely adaptable; they are immortal; see 138 423, VI 344 433.

In arms not worse, in foresight much advanced,
We may with more successful hope resolve   120
To wage by force or guile eternal war
Irreconcilable to our grand Foe,
Who now triumphs, and in the excess of joy
Sole reigning holds the tyranny of heaven.

So spake the apostate angel, though in pain,   125
Vaunting aloud, but racked with deep despair:
And him thus answered soon his bold compeer.

O prince, O chief of many thronèd powers
That led the embattled seraphim to war
Under thy conduct, and in dreadful deeds   130
Fearless, endangered heaven's perpetual King;
And put to proof his high supremacy,
Whether upheld by strength, or chance, or fate,
Too well I see and rue the dire event,
That with sad overthrow and foul defeat   135
Hath lost us heaven, and all this mighty host
In horrible destruction laid thus low,
As far as gods and heavenly essences
Can perish: for the mind and spirit remains
Invincible, and vigour soon returns,   140
Though all our glory extinct, and happy state
Here swallowed up in endless misery.
But what if he our Conqueror, (whom I now
Of force believe almighty, since no less
Than such could have o'erpowered such force as   145
    ours)
Have left us this our spirit and strength entire

Empyréal or empýreal.   122 Foe another way of not naming God.
125 apostate having deserted, especially from a religion.   128 thronèd
powers angels in general.   130 conduct leadership   131 perpetual
sneer at the changelessness of heaven.   133 B attributes God's supremacy to pagan forces: Christianity has always denied power, chance and
fate as ultimate realities.   141 extinct extinguished; the glory is
especially their brightness.   146 entire whole, undamaged – the

Strongly to suffer and support our pains,
That we may so suffice his vengeful ire,
Or do him mightier service as his thralls
By right of war, whate'er his business be   150
Here in the heart of hell to work in fire,
Or do his errands in the gloomy deep;
What can it then avail though yet we feel
Strength undiminished, or eternal being
To undergo eternal punishment?   155

Whereto with speedy words the arch-fiend replied.
Fallen cherub, to be weak is miserable
Doing or suffering: but of this be sure,
To do aught good never will be our task,
But ever to do ill our sole delight,   160
As being the contrary to his high will
Whom we resist. If then his providence
Out of our evil seek to bring forth good,
Our labour must be to pervert that end,
And out of good still to find means of evil;   165
Which oft-times may succeed, so as perhaps
Shall grieve him, if I fail not, and disturb
His inmost counsels from their destined aim.
But see the angry Victor hath recalled
His ministers of vengeance and pursuit   170
Back to the gates of heaven: the sulphurous hail
Shot after us in storm, o'erblown hath laid
The fiery surge, that from the precipice
Of heaven received us falling, and the thunder,

better to suffer pain, he suggests. Rhymes ire, fire. **152 deep** chaos.
154 being existence. **158 Doing or suffering** whether in action or
enduring. Parody of the two kinds of religious life, active or contemplative.
162–3 This is what God's providence does: XII 470 ' all this good [Christ's
redemption of man] of evil shall produce, and evil turn to good'. For
Satan's nihilism see IV 110 'Evil be thou my good' and IX 477, *PR* III 209.
167 If I fail not if I'm not mistaken – colloquial. **168 counsels**
plans, providence. **170 ministers** angels. **172 laid** calmed. M
has to slacken the inconveniences of hell to let the devils act; cf. 210.
173–4 Topsyturvy syntax is mimetic.

Winged with red lightning and impetuous rage,   175
Perhaps hath spent his shafts, and ceases now
To bellow through the vast and boundless deep.
Let us not slip the occasion, whether scorn,
Or satiate fury yield it from our Foe.
Seest thou yon dreary plain, forlorn and wild,   180
The seat of desolation, void of light,
Save what the glimmering of these livid flames
Casts pale and dreadful? Thither let us tend
From off the tossing of these fiery waves,
There rest, if any rest can harbour there,   185
And reassembling our afflicted powers,
Consult how we may henceforth most offend
Our Enemy, our own loss how repair,
How overcome this dire calamity,
What reinforcement we may gain from hope,   190
If not what resolution from despair.

          Thus Satan talking to his nearest mate
With head up-lift above the wave, and eyes
That sparkling blazed, his other parts besides
Prone on the flood, extended long and large   195
Lay floating many a rood, in bulk as huge
As whom the fables name of monstrous size,
Titanian, or Earth-born, that warred on Jove,
Briáreos or Typhon, whom the den

176 **his** the thunder's; M avoided *its*.   178 **slip** miss.   183 **tend** move.
186 **powers** troops.   191 **despair** anti-rhyme with hope, cf. II 6.
Satan's speeches, and hell's landscape, formed of contradictions and
negatives. Hope is one of the theological virtues, despair the final
vice: hence Hopkins *Carrion comfort*. Complexity of this speech
characteristic of *PL* I–II; 'vicious syntax' Bentley called it here.
193 **head up-lift** like a seasnake, as finally at x 531 'huge Python'. His
other parts seem dislocated.   196 **rood** rod, pole or perch.   197 **As
whom** as those whom. Introduces the first epic simile; one of several
formulas. M disparages classical myth as fable – cf. 580 746 – as against
Christian truth. The issue of earth (Ge) included gigantic Titans, and
serpentine monsters such as Briareus and Typhon (Typhoeus) who
rebelled against divine parents or rulers and were shut under volcanoes
for it.

By ancient Tarsus held, or that sea-beast   200
Leviathan, which God of all his works
Created hugest that swim the ocean stream:
Him haply slumbering on the Norway foam
The pilot of some small night-foundered skiff,
Deeming some island, oft, as seamen tell,   205
With fixèd anchor in his scaly rind
Moors by his side under the lea, while night
Invests the sea, and wishèd morn delays:
So stretched out huge in length the arch-fiend lay
Chained on the burning lake, nor ever thence   210
Had risen or heaved his head, but that the will
And high permission of all-ruling Heaven
Left him at large to his own dark designs,
That with reiterated crimes he might
Heap on himself damnation, while he sought   215
Evil to others, and enraged might see
How all his malice served but to bring forth
Infinite goodness, grace and mercy shown
On man by him seduced, but on himself
Treble confusion, wrath and vengeance poured.   220
Forthwith upright he rears from off the pool
His mighty stature; on each hand the flames
Driven backward slope their pointing spires, and rolled
In billows leave i' the midst a horrid vale.
Then with expanded wings he steers his flight   225
Aloft, incumbent on the dusky air
That felt unusual weight, till on dry land
He lights, if it were land that ever burned

200 **Tarsus** capital of Cilicia, where Typhon had his lair; also where Paul came from, so shifts classics to Bible.   201 **Leviathan** mythically, chaos or Satan; actually, crocodile or whale. What is simile's effect? 202 'Accents very absonous' Bentley; cf. VII 412. **Ocean stream** translates Homeric Greek for water that rings the earth's disc; or Atlantic.   203 'It must be very solid foam that can support a sleeping whale' Bentley.   204 **Pilot** skipper. **night-foundered** sunk in night. 208 **Invests** wraps; besieges.   209 Changes rhythm, and repeats 196 to frame simile.   221 Effortful rhythm.   226 **incumbent on** leaning his weight on – common usage but hinting at the incubus, which lies with sleeping women? In prose M punned incumbent=priest=devil.

58

With solid, as the lake with liquid fire;
And such appeared in hue, as when the force   230
Of subterranean wind transports a hill
Torn from Pelorus, or the shattered side
Of thundering Ætna, whose combustible
And fuelled entrails thence conceiving fire,
Sublimed with mineral fury, aid the winds,   235
And leave a singèd bottom all involved
With stench and smoke: such resting found the sole
Of unblessed feet. Him followed his next mate,
Both glorying to have scaped the Stygian flood
As gods, and by their own recovered strength,   240
Not by the sufferance of supernal Power.

Is this the region, this the soil, the clime,
Said then the lost archangel, this the seat
That we must change for heaven, this mournful gloom
For that celestial light? Be it so, since he   245
Who now is sovereign can dispose and bid
What shall be right: farthest from him is best
Whom reason hath equalled, force hath made supreme
Above his equals. Farewell happy fields
Where joy for ever dwells: hail horrors, hail   250

230 **And such** ... and its colour and texture were like volcanic ash. Earthquakes and eruptions thought to be caused by underground winds as if earth were a great bowel whose contents ignite on exposure to the air, sublime directly from solid to gas, and so add more explosions. Satan himself seen as a mountain at IV 987, and often as anal.   232 **Pelorus** near Etna in Sicily; the Giant Enceladus buried there *Aeneid* III 570. 235 **mineral fury** underground pressure.   236 **bottom** hollow; here, crater. Not vulgar till late 18c. **involved** wreathed.   238 **feet** from God's curse on the Israelites should they disobey him, 'neither shall the sole of thy foot have rest' *Deut.* xxviii. Cf. Christ's feet in Blake's *Jerusalem*, Eliot's *Sunday morning service*.   239 **Stygian** hellish, from the Styx which flowed round Tartarus.   240 **gods** angels – they're still angels, of a sort; but the word also relates them to paganism again. 244 **change** exchange.   245 **Be it so** amen.   246 **dispose and bid** arrange and command. Implying it's only right because God says it is; and then putting God into the position of mere victor: although by rights we are all equal, by force he is supreme.   249 **happy fields** the Elysian Fields were a heavenly island in Homer. S performs an ancient

Infernal world, and thou profoundest hell
Receive thy new possessor: one who brings
A mind not to be changed by place or time.
The mind is its own place, and in itself
Can make a heaven of hell, a hell of heaven.   255
What matter where, if I be still the same,
And what I should be, all but less than he
Whom thunder hath made greater? Here at least
We shall be free; the Almighty hath not built
Here for his envy, will not drive us hence: 260
Here we may reign secure, and in my choice
To reign is worth ambition though in hell:
Better to reign in hell, than serve in heaven.
But wherefore let we then our faithful friends,
The associates and co-partners of our loss   265
Lie thus astonished on the oblivious pool,
And call them not to share with us their part
In this unhappy mansion, or once more
With rallied arms to try what may be yet
Regained in heaven, or what more lost in hell?   270

So Satan spake, and him Beelzebub
Thus answered. Leader of those armies bright,
Which but the Omnipotent none could have foiled,
If once they hear that voice, their liveliest pledge
Of hope in fears and dangers, heard so oft   275

ritual of victims and poets, *ave atque vale*. **256 What matter**... what
does it matter where I am so long as I stay the same, and stay what I
should be? then with 'all but less than' his syntax collapses. **260 Here**
very heavily stressed and part of a series of repetitive figures; introduces
the rumour of God's new creation, which S is also jealous of. 'Chains in
hell, not realms expect' is Abdiel's reply vi 186. **265 loss** not usually
what you go into partnership for. The word echoes in this area, from 4.
266 astonished thunderstruck. **oblivious** unconscious, as with concus-
sion or drug. In the classical hell Lethe was river of forgetfulness; but the
fallen angels are 'reserved to more wrath' 54. At 280 it's a lake of fire
again; M's topography muddled. **268 mansion** place; 'In my
Father's house are many mansions'; 'Hell itself will pass away And leave
her dolorous mansions to the peering day' *NO*. **274 liveliest pledge**
most vital assurance.

In worst extremes, and on the perilous edge
Of battle when it raged, in all assaults
Their surest signal, they will soon resume
New courage and revive, though now they lie
Grovelling and prostrate on yon lake of fire,   280
As we erewhile, astounded and amazed,
No wonder, fallen such a pernicious highth.

He scarce had ceased when the superior fiend
Was moving toward the shore; his ponderous shield
Ethereal temper, massy, large and round,   285
Behind him cast; the broad circumference
Hung on his shoulders like the moon, whose orb
Through optic glass the Tuscan artist views
At evening from the top of Fésolè,
Or in Valdarno, to descry new lands,   290
Rivers or mountains in her spotty globe.
His spear, to equal which the tallest pine
Hewn on Norwegian hills, to be the mast
On some great ammiral, were but a wand,
He walked with to support uneasy steps   295
Over the burning marl, not like those steps
On heaven's azure, and the torrid clime
Smote on him sore besides, vaulted with fire;
Nathless he so endured, till on the beach
Of that inflamèd sea, he stood and called   300

276 edge front line. Rhyme.   **282 pernicious** destructive. B's tone
rather chatty in spite of long words.   **283 superior** higher or lower?
Tense shifts.   **284 ponderous** heavy. Sentence = 'His shield, which was
made in heaven, of heavenly metal and force....hung behind him'; the
clauses pile up to mime accoutred weight. Shields symbolize their bearer,
his world or values; hence heraldry, and long description of Achilles'
shield in *Iliad*. Satan's shield transcends all others by taking in the solar
system.   **288 artist** scientist. Galileo the first man to see moon through a
telescope (optic glass: normal usage) strong enough to resolve its features;
described its uneven surface in *Siderius nuncius* Venice 1610; Inquisition
confined him for heresy. M claims to have visited him 1638 during Italian
tour. That was near Florence, in valley of river Arno, among the hills of
Fiesole in Tuscany. G went blind at this time.   **294 ammiral** flagship.
This part of the simile suggests giants, and values opposed to Galileo's.
299 Nathless none the less. Feet again.

His legions, angel forms, who lay entranced
Thick as autumnal leaves that strow the books
In Vallombrosa, where the Etrurian shades
High overarched embower; or scattered sedge
Afloat, when with fierce winds Orion armed   305
Hath vexed the Red Sea coast, whose waves o'erthrew
Busiris and his Memphian chivalry,
While with perfidious hatred they pursued
The sojourners of Goshen, who beheld
From the safe shore their floating carcasses   310
And broken chariot wheels, so thick bestrown
Abject and lost lay these, covering the flood,
Under amazement of their hideous change.
He called so loud, that all the hollow deep
Of hell resounded. Princes, potentates,   315
Warriors, the flower of heaven, once yours, now lost,
If such astonishment as this can seize
Eternal spirits; or have ye chosen this place
After the toil of battle to repose
Your wearied virtue, for the ease you find   320
To slumber here, as in the vales of heaven?
Or in this abject posture have ye sworn
To adore the Conqueror? who now beholds

303 **Vallombrosa** tree-filled valley near Florence; literally, valley of the
shadow. Etrurian = Tuscan. Dead leaves almost archetypal image for the
hosts of dead: *Isaiah* xxxiv, *Iliad* vi 146, *Aeneid* vi 309, *Inferno* iii 112.
304 **sedge** Red Sea was called Sea of Sedge in Hebrew. Storms tear up the
weed at seasons when the constellation of Orion (marked by a tilted row of
stars like a sword-belt) rises. Orion originally a giant hunter: see his myth.
For other wind-star similes cf. 594, ii 707, x 449. At *Job* ix and *Amos* v
Orion stands for God's power to control the seasons – as when he let the
Israelites over the Red Sea and drowned the pursuing Egyptians *Exodus*
xiv. The simile also hints at the flood xi 739. Busiris is an incorrect name
for the pharaoh then, perfidious because he had let them go and then
reneged. Goshen: where the Israelites were held captive in Egypt.
Memphian chivalry = Egyptian cavalry: sneer at chivalric romance.
311 **so thick** frames simile and returns to fallen angels, as 'so loud' does
for Satan and the whole series.   312 **Abject** thrown down. Lost again:
cf. 265. Perhaps abjéct here.   313 **amazement** still stupefied by their
hideous fall from heaven to hell, angel to devil; cf. astonishment 317.
316 **flower** chivalric word for pick. Sarcasm makes syntax ambiguous.
320 **virtue** manhood.

Cherub and seraph rolling in the flood
With scattered arms and ensigns, till anon   325
His swift pursuers from heaven gates discern
The advantage, and descending tread us down
Thus drooping, or with linkèd thunderbolts
Transfix us to the bottom of this gulf.
Awake, arise, or be for ever fallen.   330

They heard, and were abashed, and up they sprung
Upon the wing, as when men wont to watch
On duty, sleeping found by whom they dread,
Rouse and bestir themselves ere well awake.
Nor did they not perceive the evil plight   335
In which they were, or the fierce pains not feel;
Yet to their general's voice they soon obeyed
Innumerable. As when the potent rod
Of Amram's son in Egypt's evil day
Waved round the coast, up called a pitchy cloud   340
Of locusts, warping on the eastern wind,
That o'er the realm of impious Pharaoh hung
Like night, and darkened all the land of Nile:
So numberless were those bad angels seen
Hovering on wing under the cope of hell   345
'Twixt upper, nether, and surrounding fires;
Till, as a signal given, the uplifted spear
Of their great sultan waving to direct
Their course, in even balance down they light
On the firm brimstone, and fill all the plain;   350
A multitude, like which the populous north
Poured never from her frozen loins, to pass

332 **wont** trained.   339 **Amram's son** Moses; ancestral name normal
in epic. One of the plagues that he called down on Egypt with his magic
rod was of locusts *Exodus* x. Locusts a common 17c metaphor for devils:
see *Revelation* ix and the insects of horror paintings.   340 **coast** land.
341 **warping** sailing up and down.   345 **cope** roof.   348 **sultan** used
in 17c of despots in general; also sneer at oriental barbarism.   352 **loins**
standing for womb; first of a series of images of unnatural generation and
sterility, cf. 505, II 624. The barbarians come like glaciers melting.
Actually they came from eastern Asia but descended on Rome in the

Rhene or the Danaw, when her barbarous sons
Came like a deluge on the south, and spread
Beneath Gibraltar to the Libyan sands.   355

　　Forthwith from every squadron and each band
The heads and leaders thither haste where stood
Their great commander; godlike shapes and forms
Excelling human, princely dignities,
And powers that erst in heaven sat on thrones;   360
Though of their names in heavenly records now
Be no memorial, blotted out and rased
By their rebellion, from the books of life.
Nor had they yet among the sons of Eve
Got them new names, till wandering o'er the earth, 365
Through God's high sufferance for the trial of man,
By falsities and lies the greatest part
Of mankind they corrupted to forsake
God their creator, and the invisible
Glory of him that made them to transform   370
Oft to the image of a brute, adorned
With gay religions full of pomp and gold,
And devils to adore for deities:
Then were they known to men by various names,
And various idols through the heathen world.   375
Say, Muse, their names then known, who first, who last,
Roused from the slumber on that fiery couch,
At their great emperor's call, as next in worth

3–4c AD from the north. The names Goth, Vandal, Hun still mean
barbarian.　　**365 new names** it was thought that all the religions of the
world other than Judaism were the worship of fallen angels who had
become pagan gods.　　**366 high sufferance** over-ruling permission, to
test man.　　**370 Glory** breathcatching hiatus at end of line before;
distinguishes God from gods; quotes *Romans* i 'changed the glory of the
incorruptible God into an image...' The objection, to all religions in
which God is likened to a man or animal, or in which an image is worshipped, stems from the first two commandments; it was the puritans'
objection to images of the Virgin, crucifixes etc.　　**372 gay religions**
tawdry rituals. The rhythm of these lines bounces. For satire on pomp
cf. 717, IV 354, XI 578, *PR* IV 110.　　**373 for** as if they were.　　**376 Say,
Muse** he calls on the muse to recite the names by which they were known
later when they had become heathen gods. This catalogue = ships *Iliad* II
484.　　**377 couch** !　　**378 worth** rank.

Came singly where he stood on the bare strand,
While the promiscuous crowd stood yet aloof?   380
   The chief were those who from the pit of hell
Roaming to seek their prey on earth, durst fix
Their seats long after next the seat of God,
Their altars by his altar, gods adored
Among the nations round, and durst abide   385
Jehovah thundering out of Sion, throned
Between the cherubim; yea, often placed
Within his sanctuary itself their shrines,
Abominations; and with cursèd things
His holy rites, and solemn feasts profaned,   390
And with their darkness durst affront his light.
First Moloch, horrid king besmeared with blood
Of human sacrifice, and parents' tears,
Though for the noise of drums and timbrels loud
Their children's cries unheard, that passed through   395
   fire
To his grim idol. Him the Ammonite
Worshipped in Rabba and her watery plain,
In Argob and in Basan, to the stream
Of utmost Arnon. Nor content with such
Audacious neighbourhood, the wisest heart   400
Of Solomon he led by fraud to build

380 promiscuous not differentiated; 'other ranks'.   **383–4** Indignant
short stresses. He starts with the gods of Palestine, who were always
seducing the Israelites. Manasseh 'built altars for all the host of heaven' in
Yahweh's temple *II Kings* xxi; for other idolatry (usual OT word is
abominations) see round *I Kings* xv. The cherubim here are the gold
figures at each end of the ark where Yahweh lived in the temple's holy
of holies.   **392 Moloch** the name means king. See introductions to I and
to II for all the peers of hell. The place-names are on the frontier of Judah
NE of the Dead Sea; they don't matter except as M's equivalent of
such details in Homer; but a 17c reader would locate them easily.
394 timbrels tambourines.   **400 neighbourhood** nearness.   **401 he**
Moloch. Solomon had 700 wives, 300 concubines; many were foreign and
for all his wisdom persuaded him when he was old to worship their gods
IKings xi. Fraud=their guile. He built altars to them on the Mt of Olives,
so it was called Mt of Corruption (opprobrious; cf. 416 443). That is across
the valley from Mt Zion, where the temple was. In the valley, Hinnom,
were the royal gardens; there he planted groves to these nature gods.

His temple right against the temple of God
On that opprobrious hill, and made his grove
The pleasant valley of Hinnom, Tophet thence
And black Gehenna called, the type of hell. 405
Next Chemos, the óbscene dread of Moab's sons,
From Ároar to Nebo, and the wild
Of southmost Ábarim; in Hesebon
And Horonaïm, Seon's realm, beyond
The flowery dale of Sibma clad with vines, 410
And Eleálè to the asphaltic pool.
Peor his other name, when he enticed
Israel in Sittim, on their march from Nile,
To do him wanton rites, which cost them woe.
Yet thence his lustful orgies he enlarged 415
Even to that hill of scandal, by the grove
Of Moloch homicide, lust hard by hate;
Till good Josiah drove them thence to hell.

  With these came they, who from the bordering flood
Of old Euphrates to the brook that parts 420
Egypt from Syrian ground, had general names
Of Baälim and Ashtaroth; those male,
These feminine. For spirits when they please
Can either sex assume, or both; so soft

When King Josiah reformed Jerusalem he turned the valley into a
rubbish-dump and its names became words for hell (type=model).
406 Next Chemos next came Chemos, the foul idol of the Moabites. They
lived SE of the Dead Sea (asphaltic pool); these places had once been
captured by the Israelites; the tone presents them as the promised land.
These Palestinian gods (baalim) each had a local cult and name: Moloch
was one, Peor another. Long before Solomon, when the Israelites were still
nomads, they stayed in a part of Moab called Shittim and learned agri-
culture there; so started to worship Peor. This included ritual copulation
with local women. Moses had the leaders killed and Yahweh sent a plague;
it was stayed when Zimri and a Moabite woman were pinned together with
a spear. But orgies in 415=merely Greek *orgia* rites.   **415 enlarged** from
that episode Peor extended his worship to Solomon, who worshipped him
as well as Moloch.   **421 Syrian** Syria was a general name for the
hinterland that curved beyond the Jordan from the earlier reaches of the
Euphrates in the NE to Sinai in the SW. Ammon, Moab, etc. were in it.
422 Ashtaroth moon goddesses of whom Ashtoreth (438) was one.
424 sex cf. VIII 620.

And uncompounded is their essence pure,   425
Not tied or manacled with joint or limb,
Nor founded on the brittle strength of bones,
Like cumbrous flesh; but in what shape they choose
Dilated or condensed, bright or obscure,
Can execute their airy purposes,   430
And works of love or enmity fulfil.
For those the race of Israel oft forsook
Their living strength, and unfrequénted left
His righteous altar, bowing lowly down
To bestial gods; for which their heads as low   435
Bowed down in battle, sunk before the spear
Of déspicable foes. With these in troop
Came Astoreth, whom the Phoenicians called
Astartè, queen of heaven, with crescent horns;
To whose bright image nightly by the moon   440
Sidonian virgins paid their vows and songs,
In Sion also not unsung, where stood
Her temple on the offensive mountain, built
By that uxorious king, whose heart though large,
Beguiled by fair idolatresses, fell   445
To idols foul. Thammuz came next behind,

425 uncompounded...essence angelic substance unmixed with anything else (as human souls are housed in the body, and the body is a
mixture of elements). **429 dilated or condensed** the good angels at
VI 597 could have escaped Satan's cannonballs 'By quick contraction or
remove' had they not been hampered by armour. At IV 986 Satan dilates
up to the sky. **obscure** dark. **433 living strength** Yahweh, as opposed
to idols. **437 in troop** trooping, perhaps with a glance at Latin
troppus = flock as in 489 and VI 857 when Christ shoos them out of heaven.
441 Sidonian Sidon was capital of Phoenicia. Ashtoreth is called queen
of heaven in the Bible because she was a moon-goddess (horns = moon
and/or cow); but perhaps M glances at nuns worshipping Mary here.
444 uxorious 'fondly overcome by female charm' like Adam. That is
why we have come back to Solomon (cf. 401): if he could fall, who not?
'Heart though large' quotes *I Kings* iv 29 but the Hebrew means intellectual range. **445 fell !** **446 Thammuz** god of sun and fertility,
Ashtoreth's consort. In the myth, he was killed by a wild boar. Ritually,
his death was mourned in Babylon when plants died in the summer heat;
later in Phoenicia he was celebrated when red mud flooding down the
river Adonis from Mt Lebanon signalled spring and suggested he died
and rose again each year. Ezekiel had a vision of Israelite women weeping

Whose annual wound in Lebanon allured
The Syrian damsels to lament his fate
In amorous ditties all a summer's day,
While smooth Adonis from his native rock   450
Ran purple to the sea, supposed with blood
Of Thammuz yearly wounded: the love-tale
Infected Sion's daughters with like heat,
Whose wanton passions in the sacred porch
Ezekiel saw, when by the vision led   455
His eye surveyed the dark idolatries
Of alienated Judah. Next came one
Who mourned in earnest, when the captive ark
Maimed his brute image, head and hands lopped off
In his own temple, on the grunsel edge,   460
Where he fell flat, and shamed his worshippers:
Dagon his name, sea monster, upward man
And downward fish; yet had his temple high
Reared in Azotus, dreaded through the coast
Of Palestine, in Gath and Ascalon,   465
And Accaron and Gaza's frontier bounds.
Him followed Rimmon, whose delightful seat

for Thammuz in the temple *Ezekiel* viii.   **451 Supposed** supposedly.
These lines are luxurious as a late Elizabethan pastoral; the next passage
is grim.   **457 ... Dagon** was corn-god and/or fish-god of the Philistines. They lived on the coast SW of Jerusalem and included Goliath and
Delilah. During the Israelites' attempts to settle Canaan they were defeated by the Philistines; to encourage themselves they brought the ark
from Shiloh, the holy place where the tabernacle was waiting, to their
camp; the Philistines attacked again and took the ark to Dagon's temple.
In the morning Dagon's image (half fish, like Caliban) had fallen down;
next morning its head and hands had broken off on the threshold (ground-
sill).   **467 Him followed Rimmon** Dagon was followed in the parade
by Rimmon (=thunderer), a sky-god worshipped in Syria. Syria stood for
decadence, and opposition to the crusaders. It lay between the rivers
Abana and Pharpar, its capital Damascus famous for roses, steel and
Paul's conversion. To bow the knee to Rimmon=palter with your conscience: Elisha cured Naaman, captain of the hosts of Syria, of his leprosy
by making him wash in Jordan; so Naaman turned to Yahweh but asked
to be allowed to bow to Rimmon when with his own king *II Kings* v.
Later King Ahaz of Judah plundered the temple to buy help against
Syria; Syria was beaten and Ahaz had a copy of the altar of Rimmon made
to displace a temple altar; cf. 384 and *II Kings* xvi.

Was fair Damascus, on the fertile banks
Of Ábbana and Pharphar, lucid streams.
He also against the house of God was bold: 470
A leper once he lost and gained a king,
Ahaz his sottish conqueror, whom he drew
God's altar to disparage and displace
For one of Syrian mode, whereon to burn
His odious offerings, and adore the gods   475
Whom he had vanquished. After these appeared
A crew who under names of old renown,
Osiris, Isis, Orus and their train
With monstrous shapes and sorceries abused
Fanatic Egypt and her priests, to seek   480
Their wandering gods disguised in brutish forms
Rather than human. Nor did Israel scape
The infection when their borrowed gold composed
The calf in Oreb: and the rebel king

472 sottish foolish. As Dagon bowed to his worshippers, Ahaz worshipped the god he had beaten.   **477 crew** company. Egyptian gods, detailed more clearly in *NO* 211. Because they were represented with animal heads or worshipped in the form of actual animals (a relic of totemism) M calls them monstrous (hybrid). The chief, Osiris, was god of the dead: bull. Isis, his sister and mate, goddess of fertility and moon: cow (cf. Ashtoreth 438 and Greek Io). Her son Horus, sun-god: hawk.   **479 abused** deceived. **481 wandering** several meanings: (a) Osiris was chopped up and scattered by his enemy Set or Typhon; Isis went about collecting his parts and putting them together. (b) In Greek myth, Typhon's father, the giant Typhoeus, chased the Olympian gods into Egypt where they hid from him in animal shape and so came to be worshipped like that: Ovid *Metamorphoses* V 315. (c) Wandering like herds instead of settled like gods and men. (d) The word often dangerous in *PL*: see elsewhere in I–II and cf. VII 20 50 302, IX 1136ff, XI 282. What matters is the desperate pursuit of deceptions, instead of rational faith in the eternal.   **482 scape** escape For worship of the golden calf see *Exodus* xxxii and *Psalm* cvi; it was Apis, a form of Osiris. The reference takes us back to Horeb, Sinai, Moses. **484 rebel king** Solomon's son Rehoboam was a tyrant; 10 of the tribes accepted Jeroboam instead so he became the 'rebel king' of Israel, leaving Rehoboam king of the other 2 tribes Judah and Benjamin; they became the kingdom of Judah. This was the 'division of the kingdom'. Judah centred on Jerusalem where the temple and ark were; to weaken its pull over his 10 tribes, Jeroboam (who had been in Egypt) set up temples to Osiris in Bethel and Dan, with golden calves to worship. He told the Israelites that these were the gods who had brought them out of Egypt. So he likened to the grass-fed ox his maker Jehovah who had killed all the first-born of

Doubled that sin in Bethel and in Dan,   485
Likening his Maker to the grazèd ox,
Jehovah, who in one night when he passed
From Egypt marching, equalled with one stroke
Both her first born and all her bleating gods.

    Belial came last, than whom a spirit more lewd   490
Fell not from heaven, or more gross to love
Vice for itself: to him no temple stood
Or altar smoked; yet who more oft than he
In temples and at altars, when the priest
Turns atheist, as did Eli's sons, who filled   495
With lust and violence the house of God.
In courts and palaces he also reigns
And in luxurious cities, where the noise
Of riot ascends above their loftiest towers,
And injury and outrage: and when night   500
Darkens the streets, then wander forth the sons
Of Belial, flown with insolence and wine.
Witness the streets of Sodom, and that night
In Gibeah, when the hospitable door
Exposed a matron to avoid worse rape.   505
    These were the prime in order and in might;
The rest were long to tell, though far renowned,

Egypt, both man and beast, but passed over the Israelites when he led
them out of Egypt *I Kings* xii, *Exodus* xii. For Christians as well as Jews
the deliverance from Egypt a model of God's defence against tyranny.
490 Belial Not really a god but a personification so no smoke of sacrifice
or incense. M uses him here as instigator of incongruous evil – impurity
in temples etc. Note indignant beats on such words as oft...In...at,
filled...lust...violence.　　**495 Eli's sons** the high priest's sons desecrated the tabernacle by lying with its maidservants; they were killed when
the Philistines captured the ark for Dagon 458; *I Samuel* ii. M has 17c
priests in mind.　　**502 flown** high. Refers to the muggers of Restoration
London who beat people up in the streets. Then shifts to Sodom as
another example: when two angels visited Lot there, the homosexuals of
the city tried to rape them, even though Lot offered them his daughters
Genesis xix. The story reflects Israelite distaste for the male and female
prostitution which was part of the religion of neighbouring peoples.
Gibeah was another city where religious prostitution was practised.
Judges xix tells of a man whose wife ran away. He fetched her back and on
the way home they stayed with an old man in Gibeah. The homosexuals
of the city clamoured to rape the husband but he gave them his wife and

The Ionian gods, of Javan's issue held
Gods, yet confessed later than Heaven and Earth
Their boasted parents; Titan Heaven's first born   510
With his enormous brood, and birthright seized
By younger Saturn, he from mightier Jove
His own and Rhea's son like measure found;
So Jove usurping reigned: these first in Crete
And Ida known, thence on the snowy top   515
Of cold Olympus ruled the middle air
Their highest heaven; or on the Delphian cliff,
Or in Dodona, and through all the bounds
Of Doric land; or who with Saturn old
Fled over Adria to the Hesperian fields,   520
And o'er the Celtic roamed the utmost isles.

   All these and more came flocking; but with looks
Down cast and damp, yet such wherein appeared
Obscure some glimpse of joy, to have found their chief
Not in despair, to have found themselves not lost   525
In loss itself; which on his countenance cast
Like doubtful hue: but he his wonted pride
Soon recollecting, with high words, that bore

they raped her to death.   **508 Ionian** Greek. The crustiness of this
passage shows M's anxiety about the Greek gods. He is trying to prove
their inferiority not only to the Christian God but to the OT as well; and
trying to prove they are devils in disguise. Christians thought all races
descended from Noah; and that the Greeks descended from his grandson
Javan *Genesis* x: i.e. the Greeks were racially subsequent to, and a branch
of, the Hebrew line. The Greeks themselves held that their ancestors were
gods, the first being Uranus and Ge (sky, earth); yet they admitted to
several generations of birth and rebellion before their true Olympian gods
(Jove = Zeus etc.) were established. How, M implies, can a god who dates
from after the creation of sky and earth be divine?   **514 Crete** Zeus was
born on Mt Ida there. The gods lived on Olympus in NE Greece, the
highest they ever got (and M anyway outsoared these mountains in the
invocation). Delphi and Dodona had oracles.   **519 Doric land** Greece.
Then we follow the expansion of Greek religion across the Adriatic to
Italy under Saturn (one of the first Italian gods to be identified with a
Greek one – Cronos); to the Celtic fields of France and Spain (Hercules
was said to be the father of the first Celt); and so *ultima Thule* as Virgil
called the British Isles.   **522 flocking** like animals cf. 489, VI 857.
527 Like back to Satan's face now. May mean that their looks, damply
glad, cast like a shadow a similar dubious look on his, and/or shaded his
face with hesitation; but he pulled himself together again.   **528 bore**

71

Semblance of worth, not substance, gently raised
Their fainting courage, and dispelled their fears.   530
Then straight commands that at the warlike sound
Of trumpets loud and clarions be upreared
His mighty standard; that proud honour claimed
Azázel as his right, a cherub tall:
Who forthwith from the glittering staff unfurled   535
The imperial ensign, which full high advanced
Shone like a meteor streaming to the wind
With gems and golden lustre rich emblazed,
Seraphic arms and trophies: all the while
Sonorous metal blowing martial sounds: 540
At which the universal host upsent
A shout that tore hell's concave, and beyond
Frighted the reign of Chaos and old Night.
All in a moment through the gloom were seen
Ten thousand banners rise into the air   545
With orient colours waving: with them rose
A forest huge of spears: and thronging helms
Appeared, and serried shields in thick array
Of depth immeasurable: anon they move
In perfect phalanx to the Dorian mood   550
Of flutes and soft recorders; such as raised

followed by a pause, then hissing stress on semblance – his words as in-
substantial as his looks. This casts doubt on *gently* etc.   **531 straight**
Satan at once commands.   **534 Azázel** chief of those evil angels who
coupled with women and brought forth giants. This was the alternative
(and at one stage only) fall story; XI 569 *I Enoch Genesis* vi. Note clustering
strong stresses. The banner parodies romances; but cf. V 588.   **536 advanced** raised. A meteor is a falling star, bright, ominous, ephemeral;
cf. II 708.   **538 emblazed** emblazoned with coats of arms and battle
honours, including actual trophies, as in the triumphal processions of
ancient and renaissance Rome.   **541 universal** entire. Many total
words here.   **542 concave** sky; hell's is a rocky roof.   **543 reign**
realm; see II 890.   **546 orient** bright. **rose** one of a series of up words
here. They are responding to the command, Azazel's flag, the trumpets,
their own shout.   **547 forest huge of spears** meanings differ as you
shift word order.   **548 serried** locked together.   **549 anon** at once.
550 perfect phalanx cube, an angelically perfected battle-square; cf. VI
552. The square was used in 17c Britain and by the ancient Spartans
(Dorians); they went into battle to flutes. Music was divided into modes
of scale and effect, e.g. Lydian soothing, Dorian steadfast.

To highth of noblest temper heroes old
Arming to battle, and in stead of rage
Deliberate valour breathed, firm and unmoved
With dread of death to flight or foul retreat;   555
Nor wanting power to mitigate and swage
With solemn touches, troubled thoughts, and chase
Anguish and doubt and fear and sorrow and pain
From mortal or immortal minds. Thus they
Breathing united force with fixèd thought   560
Moved on in silence to soft pipes that charmed
Their painful steps o'er the burnt soil; and now
Advanced in view they stand, a horrid front
Of dreadful length and dazzling arms, in guise
Of warriors old with ordered spear and shield,   565
Awaiting what command their mighty chief
Had to impose: he through the armèd files
Darts his experienced eye, and soon travérse
The whole battalion views, their order due,
Their visages and stature as of gods,   570
Their number last he sums. And now his heart
Distends with pride, and hardening in his strength
Glories: for never since created man,

552 **temper** composure; and like tempered steel. 554 **Deliberate**
controlled. It is still the music which inspired with its breath, and did not
lack power to soothe and assuage. Note march of 'Thus they'.
560 **Breathing** sound of soldiers as they march unspeaking? At *Iliad* III 8
the Akaians march in silence breathing courage. 563 **view** review
order. They have spread out from the square into a rank bristling with
arms. M uses military jargon of the 17c. 564 **guise** they only seem
like heroes? Their arms are ordered as it would mean now; but at 569
order is used more generally – muddle? 568 **traverse** side to side of
the whole formation. 573 **Glories** colossal stress. For never since man
was created has any army been assembled which, compared with these,
would count as more than pigmies – even if all the Giants who fought
against the Olympian gods in the Phlegraean fields were joined to the heroes
who fought at Thebes and Troy, and the gods who helped on either side,
and the famous deeds of Arthur and his knights in Britain and Brittany, and
all the Arabs from Bizerta and the crusaders who fought against them,
including Charlemagne and all the knights of France. The catalogue rolls
through the 'matter' of all previous western epics and romances with a
series of deep breaths ending on the rhyming -yond and fell! So the devils
are brought up to date, and back to the subject of the poem.

Met such embodied force, as named with these
Could merit more than that small infantry   575
Warred on by cranes: though all the giant brood
Of Phlegra with the heroic race were joined
That fought at Thebes and Ilium, on each side
Mixed with auxiliar gods; and what resounds
In fable or romance of Uther's son   580
Begirt with British and Armoric knights;
And all who since, baptized or infidel
Jousted in Aspramont or Montalban,
Damasco, or Marocco, or Trebisond,
Or whom Bizerta sent from Afric shore   585
When Charlemagne with all his peerage fell
By Fontarabbia. Thus far these beyond
Compare of mortal prowess, yet observed
Their dread commander: he above the rest
In shape and gesture proudly eminent   590
Stood like a tower; his form had yet not lost
All her original brightness, nor appeared
Less than arch angel ruined, and the excess
Of glory obscured: as when the sun new risen
Looks through the horizontal misty air   595
Shorn of his beams, or from behind the moon
In dim eclipse disastrous twilight sheds
On half the nations, and with fear of change
Perplexes monarchs. Darkened so, yet shone
Above them all the arch angel: but his face   600
Deep scars of thunder had entrenched, and care
Sat on his faded cheek, but under brows
Of dauntless courage, and considerate pride
Waiting revenge: cruel his eye, but cast

587 **Thus far**. . . even though they were so far beyond comparison. . . still
they obeyed Satan; or, he went on inspecting them.   591 **tower** symbol
of God in Bible, e.g. *II Samuel* xxii. Tentative wording – not. . . nor. . .
less; *yet passim*.   595 **horizontal** at dawn the sun shines along the
atmosphere instead of through it, hence the red disc like a haloless angel.
Eclipse has opposite effect, headless corona; thought to portend disaster
(Latin *aster* star), especially change of king. These lines nearly cut by
Charles II's censor.   603 **considerate** studious.   604 **cast** shed.

Signs of remorse and passion to behold   605
The fellows of his crime, the followers rather
(Far other once beheld in bliss) condemned
For ever now to have their lot in pain,
Millions of spirits for his fault amerced
Of heaven, and from eternal splendours flung   610
For his revolt, yet faithful how they stood,
Their glory withered. As when heaven's fire
Hath scathed the forest oaks, or mountain pines,
With singèd top their stately growth though bare
Stands on the blasted heath. He now prepared   615
To speak; whereat their doubled ranks they bend
From wing to wing, and half enclose him round
With all his peers: attention held them mute.
Thrice he essayed, and thrice in spite of scorn,
Tears such as angels weep, burst forth: at last   620
Words interwove with sighs found out their way.

   O myriads of immortal spirits, O powers
Matchless, but with the Almighty, and that strife
Was not inglorious, though the event was dire,
As this place testifies, and this dire change   625
Hateful to utter: but what power of mind
Foreseeing or preságing, from the depth
Of knowledge past or present, could have feared,
How such united force of gods, how such
As stood like these, could ever know repulse?   630
For who can yet believe, though after loss,
That all these puissant legions, whose exile
Hath emptied heaven, shall fail to re-ascend
Self-raised, and repossess their native seat?
For me be witness all the host of heaven,   635
If counsels different, or danger shunned

Recurring word here. **606 fellows** companions. **609 amerced**
deprived. **611 yet** he wept to see them, and to see how faithfully they
still stood (FAITHFUL to him; FLUNG from God). **635 For me** as for me, I
swear before all angels that our defeat was not due to my failing to take
advice, or avoiding danger.

By me, have lost our hopes. But he who reigns
Monarch in heaven, till then as one secure
Sat on his throne, upheld by old repute,
Consent or custom, and his regal state   640
Put forth at full, but still his strength concealed,
Which tempted our attempt, and wrought our fall.
Henceforth his might we know, and know our own
So as not either to provoke, or dread
New war, provoked; our better part remains   645
To work in close design, by fraud or guile
What force effected not: that he no less
At length from us may find, who overcomes
By force, hath overcome but half his foe.
Space may produce new worlds; whereof so rife   650
There went a fame in heaven that he ere long
Intended to create, and therein plant
A generation, whom his choice regard
Should favour equal to the sons of heaven:
Thither, if but to pry, shall be perhaps   655
Our first eruption, thither or elsewhere:
For this infernal pit shall never hold
Celestial spirits in bondage, nor the abyss
Long under darkness cover. But these thoughts
Full counsel must mature: peace is despaired,   660
For who can think submission? War then, war
Open or understood must be resolved.

He spake: and to confirm his words, out-flew
Millions of flaming swords, drawn from the thighs
Of mighty cherubim; the sudden blaze   665
Far round illumined hell; highly they raged

640 state pomp, as opposed to power.   **644 provoke** we know enough
about his power and ours not to provoke him or, if he provokes us,
dread him. Brinkmanship. All the same, our best plan is secrecy.
650 Space very early use in this sense. S trying to avoid saying God
may create; but goes on to say a rumour was rife about that in heaven.
662 understood undeclared; cold war.   **666 highly** with intoxicated
arrogance. They respond as Roman soldiers did to a general's speech.

Against the Highest, and fierce with graspèd arms
Clashed on their sounding shields the din of war,
Hurling defiance toward the vault of heaven.

There stood a hill not far whose grisly top   670
Belched fire and rolling smoke; the rest entire
Shone with a glossy scurf, undoubted sign
That in his womb was hid metallic ore,
The work of sulphur. Thither winged with speed
A numerous brígad hastened. As when bands   675
Of pioneers with spade and pickaxe armed
Forerun the royal camp, to trench a field,
Or cast a rampart. Mammon led them on,
Mammon, the least erected spirit that fell
From heaven, for even in heaven his looks and   680
     thoughts
Were always downward bent, admiring more
The riches of heaven's pavement, trodden gold,
Than aught divine or holy else enjoyed
In vision beätific: by him first
Men also, and by his suggestion taught,   685
Ransacked the centre, and with impious hands
Rifled the bowels of their mother earth
For treasures better hid. Soon had his crew

669 heaven actually, as 658 says, they are underneath chaos.
674 sulphur thought to produce metals. Scurf was a technical term for
the flakiness of sulphurous substances; also part of a series of organic
images, cf. 352. In 17c mining was still regarded as incest of Mother
Earth. Ovid said mining began the Age of Iron, the fallen world, cf. 686.
His womb because mountains male, or M hesitating to realize the image?
675 numerous brígad large brigade; cf. soldier simile 332.   **678 cast**
throw up.   **679 Least erected** as opposed to uprightness of Adam and
Eve IV 288 and even the up-motifs of hell so far; he looks down not only
morally but like an animal, hence non-rational.   **680** Colloquial – for
even *in* heaven. . . Avarice in heaven illogical but M probably sniping at
17c priests and princes.   **683 else** than any other divine or holy thing
that can be enjoyed in the blessed sight of heaven. The beatific vision was
medieval name for sight of heaven or God, enjoyed only by angels and
dead saints, or mystics. M may be sneering at mystics' motives, or Roman
catholic emphasis on mysticism.   **686 centre** of the earth.

Opened into the hill a spacious wound
And digged out ribs of gold. Let none admire   690
That riches grow in hell; that soil may best
Deserve the precious bane. And here let those
Who boast in mortal things, and wondering tell
Of Babel, and the works of Memphian kings,
Learn how their greatest monuments of fame,   695
And strength and art are easily outdone
By spirits reprobate, and in an hour
What in an age they with incessant toil
And hands innumerable scarce perform.

Nigh on the plain in many cells prepared,   700
That underneath had veins of liquid fire
Sluiced from the lake, a second multitude
With wondrous art founded the massy ore,
Severing each kind, and scummed the bullion dross:
A third as soon had formed within the ground   705
A various mould, and from the boiling cells
By strange conveyance filled each hollow nook,
As in an organ from one blast of wind
To many a row of pipes the sound-board breathes.
Anon out of the earth a fabric huge   710
Rose like an exhalation, with the sound
Of dulcet symphonies and voices sweet,
Built like a temple, where pilasters round
Were set, and Doric pillars overlaid

689 wound parodies Christ's side wounded on cross; Adam's side opened for rib that makes Eve VIII 467; and lifegiving vagina of which both those are versions. Mammon makes love into money. Rib also then = seam of ore. **690 admire** wonder. Metaphor in *grow* still used, e.g. growth stock. Capitalism of this kind began for England in 17c.   **694 Memphian** Egyptian, from Memphis, i.e. Cairo: pyramids and Tower of Babel emblems of hubris, cf. XII 38.   **696 art** technology.   **702 sluiced** led by sluices, like a canal.   **703 founded** melted the bulk ore, as in a foundry; in doing this they separated the different metals out and skimmed the dross off the molten metal.   **706 various** complex.   **707 strange** ingenious, as instant moulding would be.   **710 Anon** instantly.   **711 exhalation** gas; shooting star or other brief sky sign; scenery of a masque; and parody of creation of earth (VII 242).   **712 symphonies** harmonies. The music links trivial masque to great temple.   **713 round** in a circle. **714 overlaid** they had architraves laid on top.

With golden architrave; nor did there want   715
Cornice or frieze, with bossy sculptures graven,
The roof was fretted gold. Not Babylon,
Nor great Alcairo such magnificence
Equalled in all their glories, to enshrine
Belus or Serapis their gods, or seat   720
Their kings, when Egypt with Assyria strove
In wealth and luxury. The ascending pile
Stood fixed her stately highth, and straight the doors
Opening their brazen folds discover wide
Within, her ample spaces, o'er the smooth   725
And level pavement: from the archèd roof
Pendent by subtle magic many a row
Of starry lamps and blazing cressets fed
With naphtha and asphaltus yielded light
As from a sky. The hasty multitude   730
Admiring entered, and the work some praise
And some the architect: his hand was known
In heaven by many a towerèd structure high,
Where sceptred angels held their residence,
And sat as princes, whom the súpreme King   735
Exalted to such power, and gave to rule,
Each in his hierarchy, the orders bright.
Nor was his name unheard or unadored

715 nor did there want nor was there lacking.   **716 bossy** knobbly in bas-relief.   **717 fretted** coffered. **Babylon** capital of Assyria with its god Belus = Baal; Alcairo capital of Egypt with its calf-god Apis: reverts to the catalogue. In Bible and 17c, Egypt and Assyria stood for all that is despotic, barbaric, heathen; and splendid. Note simile's form: they compete equally but are outdone by hell.   **722 pile** edifice. At its appointed height it stops rising, the doors immediately open themselves and reveal – a flat vacancy!   **727 magic** 'I always like this, it is mystical' – Tennyson. But why was magic needed? Perhaps the lamps hang unsupported like imitation stars 'as from a sky': more parody of creation. There are two kinds of lamp: lumps of asphalt in iron baskets called cressets; and naphtha, oil of asphalt, burning in lamps (as used on early bicycles). These substances are defiled in *PL* because they come from pitch and are supposed to bubble out of hell 340, x 298, xi 731. **733** Rhythm runs swiftly up.   **737 hierarchy** the 9 orders of angels; perhaps an unfortunately rigid emphasis on heaven's feudalism? **738 name** the architect's. M makes us grope for the myth: Ausonian was Greek for Italian. Roman Mulciber or Vulcan = Greek Hephaistos, god

79

In ancient Greece; and in Ausonian land
Men called him Mulciber; and how he fell   740
From heaven, they fabled, thrown by angry Jove
Sheer o'er the crystal battlements; from morn
To noon he fell, from noon to dewy eve,
A summer's day; and with the setting sun
Dropped from the zenith like a falling star,   745
On Lemnos the Ægæan isle: thus they relate,
Erring; for he with this rebellious rout
Fell long before; nor aught availed him now
To have built in heaven high towers; nor did he scape
By all his engines, but was headlong sent   750
With his industrious crew to build in hell.

  Meanwhile the wingèd heralds by command
Of sovereign power, with awful ceremony
And trumpets' sound throughout the host proclaim
A solemn council forthwith to be held   755
At Pandæmonium, the high capital
Of Satan and his peers: their summons called
From every band and squarèd regiment
By place or choice the worthiest; they anon
With hundreds and with thousands trooping came   760
Attended: all accéss was thronged, the gates
And porches wide, but chief the spacious hall
(Though like a covered field, where champions bold
Wont ride in armed, and at the soldan's chair
Defied the best of paynim chivalry   765
To mortal combat or career with lance)

of fire and metalsmiths. He built all the gods' palaces on Olympus. When
he interfered in a quarrel in heaven, Zeus threw him out. Note plays on
fall and similar words.   **747 Erring** devastating stress especially with
M's rolled *r*. He means the myth is a travesty of fall of angels.
750 engines inventions.   **751 industrious** working-class. Distaste for
industrialism has always been difficult to separate from snobbery about the
people who work the machines.   **753 awful** awesome.   **756 Pandemonium** παν + δαιμων + ιον = all demon assembly.   M's invention.
759 By place or choice appointed or elected.   **763 Though like**...
crowded even though it was big as a roofed field, or lists for tournaments.
764 soldan sultan, ruler of the local paynim, i.e. pagan Saracens, Arab
foes of the crusaders who here joust against them either *à l'outrance* or

Thick swarmed, both on the ground and in the air,
Brushed with the hiss of rustling wings. As bees
In spring time, when the sun with Taurus rides,
Pour forth their populous youth about the hive   770
In clusters; they among fresh dews and flowers
Fly to and fro, or on the smoothèd plank,
The suburb of their straw-built citadel,
New rubbed with balm, expatiate and confer
Their state affairs. So thick the airy crowd   775
Swarmed and were straitened; till the signal given,
Behold a wonder! they but now who seemed
In bigness to surpass Earth's giant sons
Now less than smallest dwarfs, in narrow room
Throng numberless, like that pygmean race   780
Beyond the Indian mount, or fairy elves,
Whose midnight revels, by a forest side
Or fountain some belated peasant sees,
Or dreams he sees, while overhead the moon
Sits arbitress, and nearer to the earth   785
Wheels her pale course, they on their mirth and dance
Intent, with jocund music charm his ear;
At once with joy and fear his heart rebounds.
Thus incorporeal spirits to smallest forms
Reduced their shapes immense, and were at large,   790
Though without number still amidst the hall
Of that infernal court. But far within

with the single gallop (career) to unseat opponent. A distracting
simile, surely? Swarmed in 767 starts a new one with onomatopoeia.
769 Taurus zodiacal sign of Bull which sun enters in April; i.e. spring.
773 straw-built hives used to be thatched or made of straw; cf. the
Little Pig's house. Entrance rubbed with herbs (balm) to attract the bees.
774 expatiate and confer walk about and discuss – as people did in the
halls of palaces and naves of churches till those edifices were specialized.
776 straitened packed. Then at a signal they make themselves small
enough to be 'at large' 790 in the hall.   **781 Indian mount** pigmies
were thought to live beyond the Himalayas (cf. 575), about 18 ins tall.
fairy elves elves are that race of fairy people who dance rings into
the grass under the full moon. Rather more malicious that Tolkien
represents them (name=nightmare), and smaller than actual fairies. *Mid.
Night's Dream* II i. Note dubiety of repeated *or*. The peasant reappears in
similes at IV 983, XII 631.   **785 arbitress** witness.

And in their own dimensions like themselves
The great seraphic lords and cherubim
In close recess and secret conclave sat   795
A thousand demi-gods on golden seats,
Frequent and full. After short silence then
And summons read, the great consult began.

795 close...conclave both phrases mean secret place, and secret council. Conclave especially a meeting of priests. Lack of punctuation seats them like the crowded dummies of a parliament or convocation. **797 Frequent and full** crowded. Perhaps frequént.   **798 summons** they read out the order which called the meeting, to establish its authority. **consult** debate.

Book II

H IGH ON A THRONE of royal state, which far
Outshone the wealth of Ormus and of Ind,
Or where the gorgeous East with richest hand
Showers on her kings barbaric pearl and gold,
Satan exalted sat, by merit raised   5
To that bad eminence; and from despair
Thus high uplifted beyond hope, aspires
Beyond thus high, insatiate to pursue
Vain war with heaven, and by success untaught
His proud imaginations thus displayed.   10

   Powers and Dominions, deities of heaven,
For since no deep within her gulf can hold
Immortal vigour, though oppressed and fallen,
I give not heaven for lost: from this descent
Celestial virtues rising, will appear   15
More glorious and more dread than from no fall,
And trust themselves to fear no second fate:
Me though just right, and the fixed laws of heaven

1 **High**...**far** in reading aloud let these directions go to extremes. High
is part of the 'up' motif, e.g. I 541–5 589 666, II 5–8 427 456 466. **state**
magnificence; or the throne's canopy.　　2 **Ormus** island in Persian gulf
famous for pearls and jewels; strategic on trade-route to India. Oriental
kings were showered with gold-dust and seed-pearl at coronation. Oriental
and barbaric motifs continue from 1. Partly an outshining of Camoens'
Lusiads, the epic of India.　　5 **sat** note hissing and rhymes 5–8. **merit** he
didn't inherit his throne, he deserved it; cf. Son VI 43; but Satan's is the
throne of hell.　　6 **bad** stronger in 17c.　　9 **success** results so far.
12 **For since** he explains why he still calls them deities, i.e. angels.
14 **I give not** I do not give heaven up as lost.　　15 **Celestial virtues**
angelic power; or perhaps the hierarchies of angels.　　16 **fall** rhyme
and internal assonance.　　17 **trust themselves** gain such confidence as
not to fear a second defeat.　　18 **Me though** starting with 'Me' and
ending with their 'full consent', S asserts his right to the throne by
original seniority in heaven (parody of divine right of James I ?); election;

Did first create your leader, next, free choice,
With what besides, in counsel or in fight,   20
Hath been achieved of merit, yet this loss
Thus far at least recovered, hath much more
Established in a safe unenvied throne
Yielded with full consent. The happier state
In heaven, which follows dignity, might draw   25
Envy from each inferior; but who here
Will envy whom the highest place exposes
Foremost to stand against the Thunderer's aim
Your bulwark, and condemns to greatest share
Of endless pain? where there is then no good   30
For which to strive, no strife can grow up there
From faction; for none sure will claim in hell
Precédence, none, whose portion is so small
Of present pain, that with ambitious mind
Will covet more. With this advantage then   35
To union, and firm faith, and firm accord,
More than can be in heaven, we now return
To claim our just inheritance of old,
Surer to prosper than prosperity
Could have assured us; and by what best way,   40
Whether of open war or covert guile,
We now debate; who can advise, may speak.

    He ceased, and next him Moloch, sceptered king
Stood up, the strongest and the fiercest spirit
That fought in heaven; now fiercer by despair: 45
His trust was with the Eternal to be deemed
Equal in strength, and rather than be less
Cared not to be at all; with that care lost

merit at war and in council; and by their getting up off the lake of fire
into Pandemonium – 'this loss thus far at least recovered': hollow syntax;
loss motif from 1.   **24 state** constitution, based on rank.   **33 none**
there is none that would covet more.   **39 Surer to prosper**... you've
never had it so bad, so the future can only be better.   **43 Moloch** speaks
clipped like a general. Style here is of old-fashioned military epic. See
introductions for all the peers.

Went all his fear: of God, or hell, or worse
He recked not, and these words thereafter spake.   50

   My sentence is for open war: of wiles,
More unexpert, I boast not: them let those
Contrive who need, or when they need, not now.
For while they sit contriving, shall the rest,
Millions that stand in arms, and longing wait   55
The signal to ascend, sit lingering here
Heaven's fugitives, and for their dwelling place
Accept this dark opprobrious den of shame,
The prison of his tyranny who reigns
By our delay? no, let us rather choose   60
Armed with hell flames and fury all at once
O'er heaven's high towers to force resistless way,
Turning our tortures into horrid arms
Against the Torturer; when to meet the noise
Of his almighty engine he shall hear   65
Infernal thunder, and for lightning see
Black fire and horror shot with equal rage
Among the angels; and his throne itself
Mixed with Tartárean sulphur, and strange fire,
His own invented torments. But perhaps   70
The way seems difficult and steep to scale
With upright wing against a higher foe.
Let such bethink them, if the sleepy drench

50 thereafter accordingly.   **51 sentence** opinion, vote.   **52 More unexpert** less experienced.   **56 sit** critics have blamed Milton for dead metaphors on sit–stand but stand in arms = ready for action; sit is the blimp's scorn for planning.   **59 his tyranny** parody of his majesty? cf. torturer 64.   **63 horrid** frightful.   **65 engine** chariot of wrath with which Son expelled them from heaven VI 749. Actually a spiritual vehicle based on vision of God borne on cherubim *Ezekiel* i, x. Moloch treats it as a machine and proposes to meet it with the 'nature' of hellfire – parody of the usual nature-*v*-art/machine stance, because hell is unnatural. **69 Tartarean** Tartarus was part of the Greek underworld reserved for the guilty dead. Sulphur volcanic as in I. Strange fire because alien to heaven, which has its own. Fire is sacred: two priests die in *Leviticus* x for using the wrong kind.   **73 Let such**... people who think it difficult should remember...that as spirits rising is natural to us, falling not.

Of that forgetful lake benumb not still,
That in our proper motion we ascend 75
Up to our native seat: descent and fall
To us is adverse. Who but felt of late
When the fierce Foe hung on our broken rear
Insulting, and pursued us through the deep,
With what compulsion and laborious flight 80
We sunk thus low? The ascent is easy then;
The event is feared; should we again provoke
Our Stronger, some worse way his wrath may find
To our destruction: if there be in hell
Fear to be worse destroyed: what can be worse 85
Than to dwell here, driven out from bliss, condemned
In this abhorrèd deep to utter woe;
Where pain of unextinguishable fire
Must exercise us without hope of end
The vassals of his anger, when the scourge 90
Inéxorably, and the torturing hour
Call us to penance? More destroyed than thus
We should be quite abolished and expire.
What fear we then? what doubt we to incense
His utmost ire? which to the highth enraged, 95
Will either quite consume us, and reduce
To nothing this essential, happier far
Than miserable to have eternal being;
Or if our substance be indeed divine,
And cannot cease to be, we are at worst 100
On this side nothing; and by proof we feel
Our power sufficient to disturb his heaven,
And with perpetual inroads to alarm,

sleepy drench huge dose of sleeping draught as for animals; drench also
=soaking. For the lake see I 266. **77 Who but felt** who didn't feel... ?
78 broken rear defeated rearguard. Military jargon; so is hung.
79 Insulting assaulting and exulting. **82 event** outcome. **83 Our
Stronger** another name for God. **89 exercise** religious discipline: he
talks of hell as if it were a monastery. **94 what doubt we** why do we
hesitate. **97 essential** angelic essence. Better be annihilated than exist
in misery for ever. But as he then guesses, they can't be abolished. See
I 423. **101 proof** experience.

Though inaccessible, his fatal throne:
Which if not victory is yet revenge.   105

    He ended frowning, and his look denounced
Desperate revenge, and battle dangerous
To less than gods. On the other side up rose
Belial, in act more graceful and humane;
A fairer person lost not heaven; he seemed   110
For dignity composed and high explóit:
But all was false and hollow; though his tongue
Dropped manna, and could make the worse appear
The better reason, to perplex and dash
Maturest counsels: for his thoughts were low;   115
To vice industrious, but to nobler deeds
Timorous and slothful: yet he pleased the ear,
And with persuasive accent thus began.

    I should be much for open war, O peers,
As not behind in hate; if what was urged   120
Main reason to persuade immediate war,
Did not dissuade me most, and seem to cast
Ominous conjecture on the whole success:
When he who most excels in fact of arms,
In what he counsels and in what excels   125
Mistrustful, grounds his courage on despair
And utter dissolution, as the scope
Of all his aim, after some dire revenge.
First, what revenge? The towers of heaven are filled
With armèd watch, that render all accéss   130

104 fatal fated to remain secure; and deadly.   **106 denounced** pro-
claimed.   **107 dangerous** sure to destroy.   **109 act** manner. **humane**
civilized, educated (17c usage).   **110 fairer person** no better-looking
angel fell from heaven.   **111 dignity** honour, high rank.   **113 manna**
honey-tongued; colloquial but also parody of the food God sent the
Israelites *Exodus* xvi, and of manna as angels' food *Psalm* lxxviii, and
metaphor for Christ the bread of life *John* vi.   **120 urged**... put
forward as the main argument for. Smooth arguing stress on *dis*suade *me
most*. He answers Moloch point by point.   **124 fact** deeds, action; i.e.
Moloch, who excels at and advises war but doubts its efficacy to do more
than get revenge.   **130 watch** guards.

Impregnable; oft on the bordering deep
Encamp their legions, or with óbscure wing
Scout far and wide into the realm of Night,
Scorning surprise. Or could we break our way
By force, and at our heels all hell should rise   135
With blackest insurrection, to confound
Heaven's purest light, yet our great Enemy
All incorruptible would on his throne
Sit unpolluted, and the ethereal mould
Incapable of stain would soon expel   140
Her mischief, and purge off the baser fire
Victorious. Thus repulsed, our final hope
Is flat despair: we must exasperate
The almighty Victor to spend all his rage,
And that must end us, that must be our cure,   145
To be no more; sad cure; for who would lose,
Though full of pain, this intellectual being,
Those thoughts that wander through eternity,
To perish rather, swallowed up and lost
In the wide womb of uncreated night,   150
Devoid of sense and motion? and who knows,
Let this be good, whether our angry Foe
Can give it, or will ever? how he can
Is doubtful; that he never will is sure.
Will he, so wise, let loose at once his ire,   155
Belike through impotence, or unaware,
To give his enemies their wish, and end
Them in his anger, whom his anger saves
To punish endless? Wherefore cease we then?

132 **obscure** dark. Their patrols into chaos make surprise attack from hell
laughable.   134 **Or could we** or even if we could.   139 **ethereal
mould** the fiery substance of God, and perhaps the good angels, would
prove immiscible with hellfire, and so be victorious.   141 **Her** its.
143 **we must** we should be bound to.   147 **intellectual being** mental
existence. Belial's syntax has wandered from war into imagination.
149 **rather** instead.   151 **sense** sensation.   152 **Let this be good**
supposing for the sake of argument that annihilation would be good.
156 **Belike** no doubt (sarcastic). **impotence** impatience (a 17c use).
159 **Wherefore**...? so why should we aim at annihilation? Those who
counsel war say that...

Say they who counsel war, we are decreed, 160
Reserved and destined to eternal woe;
Whatever doing, what can we suffer more,
What can we suffer worse? Is this then worst,
Thus sitting, thus consulting, thus in arms?
What when we fled amain, pursued and strook 165
With heaven's afflicting thunder, and besought
The deep to shelter us? this hell then seemed
A refuge from those wounds: or when we lay
Chained on the burning lake? that sure was worse.
What if the breath that kindled those grim fires 170
Awaked should blow them into sevenfold rage
And plunge us in the flames? or from above
Should intermitted vengeance arm again
His red right hand to plague us? what if all
Her stores were opened, and this firmament 175
Of hell should spout her cataracts of fire,
Impendent horrors, threatening hideous fall
One day upon our heads; while we perhaps
Designing or exhorting glorious war,
Caught in a fiery tempest shall be hurled 180
Each on his rock transfixed, the sport and prey
Of racking whirlwinds, or for ever sunk
Under yon boiling ocean, wrapped in chains;
There to converse with everlasting groans,
Unréspited, unpitied, unreprieved, 185
Ages of hopeless end; this would be worse.
War therefore, open or concealed, alike
My voice dissuades; for what can force or guile
With him, or who deceive his mind, whose eye
Views all things at one view? he from heaven's highth 190

173 **intermitted** the cascade of fire had stopped I 171. **174 red right hand** translates a phrase Horace used of Zeus *Odes* I ii. A similar incongruity VI 762. **175 firmament** roof. Does M have stalactites in mind? **180** Catalogue of traditional tortures of hell, so far escaped but rehearsed at 596. They seem to derive from curing and cooking meat. Is the fantasy of hell a punishment for turning carnivorous? **186 hopeless end** no end to hope for. **188 for what can...?** for what can force or guile do against him?

All these our motions vain, sees and derides;
Not more almighty to resist our might
Than wise to frústrate all our plots and wiles.
Shall we then live thus vile, the race of heaven
Thus trampled, thus expelled to suffer here   195
Chains and these torments? Better these than worse
By my advice; since fate inevitable
Subdues us, and omnipotent decree,
The Victor's will. To suffer, as to do,
Our strength is equal, nor the law unjust   200
That so ordains: this was at first resolved,
If we were wise, against so great a foe
Contending, and so doubtful what might fall.
I laugh, when those who at the spear are bold
And venturous, if that fail them, shrink and fear   205
What yet they know must follow, to endure
Exile, or ignominy, or bonds, or pain,
The sentence of their conqueror: this is now
Our doom; which if we can sustain and bear,
Our súpreme Foe in time may much remit   210
His anger, and perhaps thus far removed
Not mind us not offending, satisfied
With what is punished; whence these raging fires
Will slacken, if his breath stir not their flames.
Our purer essence then will overcome   215
Their noxious vapour, or inured not feel,
Or changed at length, and to the place conformed
In temper and in nature, will receive
Familiar the fierce heat, and void of pain;

191 **motions** plans. 'The Lord shall have them in derision' *Psalm* ii; he
does III 80, x 616.   194 **thus vile** as vile as our present state.   199 **suffer**
. . . **do** our ability to suffer is equal to our strength to attack. B seems to
base this on some law of angelic nature; then says they must have considered it when they first decided to attack God (but few editors risk
construing these lines).   204 Now he sneers at Moloch.   207 **ignominy** pronounced ígnomy by M.   212 **Not mind** take no notice of us
if we don't offend him. Probably means God will be satisfied with their
punishment so far.   216 **vapour** hot fumes.   218 **temper** . . . **nature**
temperament, balance of the humours; and physiological constitution.
219 **Familiar** accept the heat as normal and so painless. The fantasy is

This horror will grow mild, this darkness light,   220
Besides what hope the never-ending flight
Of future days may bring, what chance, what change
Worth waiting, since our present lot appears
For happy though but ill, for ill not worst,
If we procure not to ourselves more woe.   225

   Thus Belial with words clothed in reason's garb
Counselled ignoble ease, and peaceful sloth,
Not peace: and after him thus Mammon spake.

   Either to disenthrone the King of heaven
We war, if war be best, or to regain   230
Our own right lost: him to unthrone we then
May hope when everlasting Fate shall yield
To fickle Chance, and Chaos judge the strife:
The former vain to hope argues as vain
The latter: for what place can be for us   235
Within heaven's bound, unless heaven's Lord supreme
We overpower? Suppose he should relent
And publish grace to all, on promise made
Of new subjection; with what eyes could we
Stand in his presence humble, and receive   240
Strict laws imposed, to celebrate his throne
With warbled hymns, and to his Godhead sing
Forced hallelujahs; while he lordly sits
Our envied Sovereign, and his altar breathes

like ours of supermen, spacemen.   **221 flight** B wanders again. In fact future days will bring mankind, Christ, Book xii.   **224 For happy**... though bad in terms of happiness, not so bad in terms of the worst. **231 him to unthrone** we can hope to dethrone God only when all order collapses. Since we can't hope for that, we can't hope to regain our own right either.   **242 warbled** Mammon is contemptuous of the court of heaven; see iii 365, v 618 653, vii 594.   **244 altar** Christ's death fulfilled the law and so made unnecessary 'those shadowy expiations weak, the blood of bulls and goats' (xii 291); yet there is a golden altar in heaven in *Revelation* vi, viii, *PL* xi 18. As in a Christian church, the offerings are prayers but there is also incense. Ambrosia is from a word meaning immortal which the Greeks used for the food and drink of their gods; it is also the name of fragrant herbs and woods; a symbol of incorruptibility, opposed to the stink of rottenness. Cf. iii 135, *PR* iv 589.

Ambrosial odours and ambrosial flowers, 245
Our servile offerings? This must be our task
In heaven, this our delight; how wearisome
Eternity so spent in worship paid
To whom we hate. Let us not then pursue
By force impossible, by leave obtained 250
Unácceptable, though in heaven, our state
Of splendid vassalage, but rather seek
Our own good from ourselves, and from our own
Live to ourselves, though in this vast recess,
Free, and to none accountable, preferring 255
Hard liberty before the easy yoke
Of servile pomp. Our greatness will appear
Then most conspicuous, when great things of small,
Useful of hurtful, prosperous of adverse
We can create, and in what place so e'er 260
Thrive under evil, and work ease out of pain
Through labour and endurance. This deep world
Of darkness do we dread? How oft amidst
Thick clouds and dark doth heaven's all-ruling Sire
Choose to reside, his glory unobscured, 265
And with the majesty of darkness round
Covers his throne; from whence deep thunders roar
Mustering their rage, and heaven resembles hell?
As he our darkness, cannot we his light
Imitate when we please? This desert soil 270
Wants not her hidden lustre, gems and gold;
Nor want we skill or art, from whence to raise
Magnificence; and what can heaven show more?

250 **by leave obtained** even if we were to be allowed it, we don't want renewed vassalage. Feudal word for a spiritual condition so Mammon condemns himself; but also satire on courts and established churches of the 17c. 254 **recess** remote place of retirement. 255 **Free** jammed between commas and pauses. 262 **world** applies to us too: 'O this gloomy world, in what a shadow and deep pit of darkness doth womanish and fearful mankind live!' Webster *Malfi* v v. Mammon's next lines quote *Psalms* xviii and xcvii on God's darkness. 270 **Imitate** begs the question of 'create' in 260. **desert** sterile. 271 **Wants not** does not lack. 272 **art** technology. Mammon led the mining for Pandemonium.

Our torments also may in length of time
Become our elements, these piercing fires   275
As soft as now severe, our temper changed
Into their temper; which must needs remove
The sensible of pain. All things invite
To peaceful counsels, and the settled state
Of order, how in safety best we may   280
Compose our present evils, with regard
Of what we are and where, dismissing quite
All thoughts of war: ye have what I advise.

He scarce had finished, when such murmur filled
The assembly, as when hollow rocks retain   285
The sound of blustering winds, which all night long
Had roused the sea, now with hoarse cadence lull
Seafaring men o'erwatched, whose bark by chance
Or pinnace anchors in a craggy bay
After the tempest: such applause was heard   290
As Mammon ended, and his sentence pleased,
Advising peace: for such another field
They dreaded worse than hell: so much the fear
Of thunder and the sword of Michaël
Wrought still within them; and no less desire   295
To found this nether empire, which might rise
By policy, and long procéss of time,
In emulation opposite to heaven.
Which when Beelzebub perceived, than whom,
Satan except, none higher sat, with grave   300
Aspéct he rose, and in his rising seemed
A pillar of state; deep on his front engraven
Deliberation sat and public care;

275 elements natural environments. Repeats Belial.   **278 sensible**
sensation.   **281 Compose** arrange.   **288 o'erwatched** exhausted
with lack of sleep. Why is the simile so vague?   **292 field** battle.
294 Michaël captain of God's army VI 250. A Hebrew name scanned here
to emphasize -el = God.   **296 nether** lower, in hell.   **297 policy** wily
statesmanship.   **299 Beelzebub** when B (who sat higher than all but
Satan) saw this, he rose, because he had already conferred with Satan
(380).   **302 front** brow or face.

And princely counsel in his face yet shone,
Majestic though in ruin: sage he stood   305
With Atlantéan shoulders fit to bear
The weight of mightiest monarchies; his look
Drew audience and attention still as night
Or summer's noontide air, while thus he spake.

   Thrones and imperial powers, offspring of   310
     heaven,
Ethereal virtues; or these titles now
Must we renounce, and changing style be called
Princes of hell? for so the popular vote
Inclines, here to continue, and build up here
A growing empire; doubtless; while we dream,   315
And know not that the King of heaven hath doomed
This place our dungeon, not our safe retreat
Beyond his potent arm, to live exempt
From heaven's high jurisdiction, in new league
Banded against his throne, but to remain   320
In strictest bondage, though thus far removed,
Under the inevitable curb, reserved
His captive multitude: for he, be sure,
In highth or depth, still first and last will reign
Sole King, and of his kingdom lose no part   325
By our revolt, but over hell extend
His empire, and with iron sceptre rule
Us here, as with his golden those in heaven.
What sit we then projecting peace and war?
War hath determined us, and foiled with loss   330

306 Atlantéan the Titan Atlas, defeated by Zeus, had to hold up the
sky. In a sonnet Spenser said Burleigh bore the state 'As the wide compass
of the firmament on Atlas' mighty shoulders is upstayed'. How straight
is Milton's allusion? **308 audience** listening. **312 style** title.
313 vote he judges by the applause for Mammon. **314 here** sarcastic
stress. **316 doomed** decreed. **326 extend** exert his rule. The iron
sceptre is from *Psalm* ii 'Thou shalt break them with a rod of iron'.
329 What sit we...? So why do we sit here...? In the 17c a project
was a fraudulent investment or a daft invention. **330 determined**
ended; we've gone as far as war will take us. **foiled** frustrated; pron. filed.

Irreparable; terms of peace yet none
Vouchsafed or sought; for what peace will be given
To us enslaved, but custody severe,
And stripes, and arbitrary punishment
Inflicted? And what peace can we return,   335
But to our power hostility and hate,
Untamed reluctance, and revenge though slow,
Yet ever plotting how the Conqueror least
May reap his conquest, and may least rejoice
In doing what we most in suffering feel?   340
Nor will occasion want, nor shall we need
With dangerous expedition to invade
Heaven, whose high walls fear no assault or siege,
Or ambush from the deep. What if we find
Some easier enterprise? There is a place   345
(If ancient and prophetic fame in heaven
Err not), another world, the happy seat
Of some new race called Man, about this time
To be created like to us, though less
In power and excellence, but favoured more   350
Of him who rules above; so was his will
Pronounced among the gods, and by an oath,
That shook heaven's whole circumference, confirmed.
Thither let us bend all our thoughts, to learn
What creatures there inhabit, of what mould,   355
Or substance, how endued, and what their power,
And where their weakness, how attempted best,
By force or subtlety: though heaven be shut,
And heaven's high Arbitrator sit secure
In his own strength, this place may lie exposed   360

332 Vouchsafed no peace treaty has so far been offered or asked for.
334 stripes whipping.   **336 to our power** to its limit.   **337 reluctance**
resistance. This is the doctrine of resistance movements.   **340 doing...**
suffering cf. 199.   **341 occasion** opportunity won't be lacking either.
346 ancient...fame long-rife rumour about the future; cf. 1 650. In *PL*
God does not fulfil the rumour till after the rebels have been expelled;
then he does it to spite and replace them VII 150, III 678 735. None of
this is Biblical.   **357 attempted** got at. B sees man in political
terms.

The utmost border of his kingdom, left
To their defence who hold it: here perhaps
Some advantageous act may be achieved
By sudden onset, either with hell fire
To waste his whole creation, or possess   365
All as our own, and drive as we were driven,
The puny habitants, or if not drive,
Seduce them to our party, that their God
May prove their foe, and with repenting hand
Abolish his own works. This would surpass   370
Common revenge, and interrupt his joy
In our confusion, and our joy upraise
In his disturbance; when his darling sons
Hurled headlong to partake with us, shall curse
Their frail original, and faded bliss,   375
Faded so soon. Advise if this be worth
Attempting, or to sit in darkness here
Hatching vain empires. Thus Beelzebub
Pleaded his devilish counsel, first devised
By Satan, and in part proposed: for whence,   380
But from the author of all ill could spring
So deep a malice, to confound the race
Of mankind in one root, and earth with hell
To mingle and involve, done all to spite
The great Creator? But their spite still serves   385
His glory to augment. The bold design
Pleased highly those infernal states, and joy

361 left... left to be defended by those who live there, i.e. men.
362 here the new world, if anywhere, is the place for Moloch's plan.
369 repenting God does regret making man when he sends the flood
Genesis vi.   **371 interrupt**... make a hole in his enjoyment of our confusion; and confuse him by sticking our enjoyment of his confusion
into the hole. Other patterns possible because the words double:
interrupt = upraise, confusion = disturbance etc.   **373 darling** favourite.
375 original origin; or Adam; or original bliss. Frail and faded hint at
fall; see Adam's garland IX 893.   **376 Advise** consider.   **378 Hatching**
parody of creating Spirit.   **382 confound** ruin. The root is Adam.
In genealogical pictures his phallus was shown as root of mankind's
family tree; so in the doctrine of 'original sin' any sin in him runs through
the race like genes or seed.   **387 states** estates; parliament.

Sparkled in all their eyes; with full assent
They vote: whereat his speech he thus renews.

Well have ye judged, well ended long debate,   390
Synod of gods, and like to what ye are,
Great things resolved, which from the lowest deep
Will once more lift us up in spite of fate,
Nearer our ancient seat; perhaps in view
Of those bright cónfines, whence with neighbouring   395
    arms
And opportune excursion we may chance
Re-enter heaven; or else in some mild zone
Dwell not unvisited of heaven's fair light
Secure, and at the brightening orient beam
Purge off this gloom; the soft delicious air,   400
To heal the scar of these corrosive fires
Shall breathe her balm. But first whom shall we send
In search of this new world, whom shall we find
Sufficient? who shall tempt with wandering feet
The dark unbottomed infinite abyss   405
And through the palpable obscure find out
His uncouth way, or spread his airy flight
Upborne with indefatigable wings
Over the vast abrupt, ere he arrive
The happy isle; what strength, what art can then   410
Suffice, or what evasion bear him safe
Through the strict senteries and stations thick

391 synod assembly, usually ecclesiastical. Pron. *sin*-erd.   **391 like** their
decision fits their greatness.   **395 cónfines** frontiers of heaven. If
they get their troops that close...Note fate, chance, if, perhaps.
400 Purge...gloom cheer their depression? or actually scrape off the
darkness?   **402** Parodies God III 213, 'Where shall we find such love?'
and *Isaiah* vi 8.   **403 world** our universe.   **404 tempt** try.   **405** The
line delays its noun to the end.   **406 palpable obscure** darkness which
may be felt like the plague in *Exodus* x.   **407 uncouth** unknown.
408 Flying rhythm, cf. VII 428.   **409 abrupt** broken off, precipitous,
used as noun for chaos. **arrive** reach.   **410 happy isle** used for
desirable places in Greek myth, and for Canaries etc., cf. III 567. Start of
series of voyaging images, cf. 636, 919, 1011, IV 159. **art** guile.
412 stations pickets. Angels here partly seen as stars.

Of angels watching round? Here he had need
All circumspection, and we now no less
Choice in our suffrage; for on whom we send,   415
The weight of all and our last hope relies.

This said, he sat; and expectation held
His look suspense, awaiting who appeared
To second, or oppose, or undertake
The perilous attempt: but all sat mute,   420
Pondering the danger with deep thoughts; and each
In other's countenance read his own dismay
Astonished: none among the choice and prime
Of those heaven-warring champions could be found
So hardy as to proffer or accept   425
Alone the dreadful voyage; till at last
Satan, whom now transcendent glory raised
Above his fellows, with monarchal pride
Conscious of highest worth, unmoved thus spake.

O progeny of heaven, empyreal thrones,   430
With reason hath deep silence and demur
Seized us, though undismayed: long is the way
And hard, that out of hell leads up to light;
Our prison strong, this huge convéx of fire,
Outrageous to devour, immures us round   435
Ninefold, and gates of burning adamant
Barred over us prohibit all egress.
These passed, if any pass, the void profound
Of unessential night receives him next
Wide gaping, and with utter loss of being   440
Threatens him, plunged in that abortive gulf.

415 choice in our suffrage care in our vote.   **417 expectation**... he
stayed looking at them expectantly.   **423 Astonished** dismayed. Their faces
mirror each other. **prime** senior. Chivalric language here.   **425 proffer**
volunteer.   **427 transcendent** can mean surpassingly excellent; but S
moves further than that, up into a sort of deity of devilry so that
he : devils :: God : man; cf. 478. Also satire on kingship; and parody of
Son's self-sacrifice III 227.   **439 unessential** non-existent.   **441 abortive**
chaos is the womb of nature 911 because the world was created out

If thence he scape into whatever world,
Or unknown region, what remains him less
Than unknown dangers and as hard escape.
But I should ill become this throne, O peers,   445
And this imperial sovereignty, adorned
With splendour, armed with power, if aught proposed
And judged of public moment, in the shape
Of difficulty or danger could deter
Me from attempting. Wherefore do I assume   450
These royalties, and not refuse to reign,
Refusing to accept as great a share
Of hazard as of honour, due alike
To him who reigns, and so much to him due
Of hazard more, as he above the rest   455
High honoured sits? Go therefore mighty powers,
Terror of heaven, though fallen; intend at home,
While here shall be our home, what best may ease
The present misery, and render hell
More tolerable; if there be cure or charm   460
To réspite or deceive, or slack the pain
Of this ill mansion: intermit no watch
Against a wakeful foe, while I abroad
Through all the coasts of dark destruction seek
Deliverance for us all: this enterprise   465
None shall partake with me. Thus saying rose
The monarch, and prevented all reply,
Prudent, lest from his resolution raised
Others among the chief might offer now
(Certain to be refused) what erst they feared;   470
And so refused might in opinion stand
His rivals, winning cheap the high repute

of its stuff; but anyone who falls into it will be reduced to nothingness, as if miscarried out of existence. Cf. what might happen to space-travellers sometimes.   **450 Wherefore**...how could I accept kingship if I refused to accept hazard? But his syntax dubious. Remember Milton's burring *r* and unsounded *h* here.   **457 Terror...fallen !** **intend** consider.   **460 charm** means to soothe or beguile (deceive). **464 coasts** regions.   **468 lest**... in case others, encouraged by his resolution, tried to cash in.

Which he through hazard huge must earn. But they
Dreaded not more the adventure than his voice
Forbidding; and at once with him they rose;   475
Their rising all at once was as the sound
Of thunder heard remote. Towards him they bend
With awful reverence prone; and as a god
Extol him equal to the highest in heaven:
Nor failed they to express how much they praised,   480
That for the general safety he despised
His own: for neither do the spirits damned
Lose all their virtue; lest bad men should boast
Their specious deeds on earth, which glory excites,
Or close ambition varnished o'er with zeal.   485
    Thus they their doubtful consultations dark
Ended rejoicing in their matchless chief:
As when from mountain tops the dusky clouds
Ascending, while the north wind sleeps, o'erspread
Heaven's cheerful face, the louring element   490
Scowls o'er the darkened landskip snow, or shower;
If chance the radiant sun with farewell sweet
Extend his evening beam, the fields revive,
The birds their notes renew, and bleating herds
Attest their joy, that hill and valley rings.   495
O shame to men! Devil with devil damned
Firm concord holds, men only disagree
Of creatures rational, though under hope
Of heavenly grace: and God proclaiming peace,
Yet live in hatred, enmity, and strife   500
Among themselves, and levy cruel wars,

---

478 awful reverent.   **483 virtue** M's point is that ethical and political
virtues such as courage and loyalty may operate in evil beings; but they
do not constitute religious virtue, or spiritual goodness. Cf. Eliot *Gerontion*
'Think: neither fear nor courage saves us'. Some virtues in any case moti-
vated by desire for glory, or secret ambition disguised as piety: 'Virtues
are forced upon us by our impudent crimes' (*Gerontion*) and *Ephesians* ii
(favourite protestant text) 'by grace are ye saved through faith...not of
works, lest any man should boast'. Crucial distinction between Christianity
and humanism.   **490 element** sky. Another weather simile; but the
gentle pastoral part depends on 'if it chances that...'

Wasting the earth, each other to destroy:
As if (which might induce us to accord)
Man had not hellish foes enow besides,
That day and night for his destruction wait.   505

    The Stygian council thus dissolved; and forth
In order came the grand infernal peers,
Midst came their mighty paramount, and seemed
Alone the antagonist of heaven, nor less
Than hell's dread emperor with pomp supreme,   510
And God-like imitated state; him round
A globe of fiery seraphim enclosed
With bright emblazonry, and horrent arms.
Then of their session ended they bid cry
With trumpets' regal sound the great result: 515
Toward the four winds four speedy cherubim
Put to their mouths the sounding alchemy
By herald's voice explained: the hollow abyss
Heard far and wide, and all the host of hell
With deafening shout returned them loud acclaim.   520
    Thence more at ease their minds and somewhat raised
By false presumptuous hope, the rangèd powers
Disband, and wandering, each his several way
Pursues, as inclination or sad choice
Leads him perplexed, where he may likeliest find   525
Truce to his restless thoughts, and entertain
The irksome hours, till his great chief return.
Part on the plain, or in the air sublime

506 **Stygian** hellish. 508 **paramount** overlord. 512 **globe** the angels
form in 3 dimensions. This imitates God's pomp III 583 and chariot VI 750,
VII 197. 513 **emblazonry...arms** heraldic shields and bristling
weapons. Romantic diction. 514 **Then**... then they bade the trumpets
announce the outcome of the parliamentary session that had just ended; a
herald explains. 517 **alchemy** a brass alloy called alchemy gold; cf.
sounding brass and tinkling cymbal *I Corinthians* xiii: hell's pageantry
is imitation. 522 **rangèd powers** armies drawn up in ranks.
523 **wandering** they are aimless, and erring. Model of neurotic drift.
several different. 528 **sublime** uplifted. Archaic usage. Heroic games a

Upon the wing, or in swift race contend,
As at the Olympian games or Pythian fields;   530
Part curb their fiery steeds, or shun the goal
With rapid wheels, or fronted brígads form.
As when to warn proud cities war appears
Waged in the troubled sky, and armies rush
To battle in the clouds, before each van   535
Prick forth the airy knights, and couch their spears
Till thickest legions close; with feats of arms
From either end of heaven the welkin burns.
Others with vast Typhœan rage more fell
Rend up both rocks and hills, and ride the air   540
In whirlwind; hell scarce holds the wild uproar.
As when Alcídès from Oechalia crowned
With conquest, felt the envenomed robe, and tore
Through pain up by the roots Thessalian pines,
And Lichas from the top of Oeta threw   545
Into the Euboic sea. Others more mild,
Retreated in a silent valley, sing

convention of epic; cf. IV 551. M compares them to historical Greek games.
The most important were held as national festivals in honour of Apollo
(the Pythian god) at Olympia every 5th year, and at Delphi.   **531 shun
the goal** steer closely round the post in a chariot race.   **532 fronted
brígads** opposing teams, for tournament.   **535 van** vanguard.
536 prick ride; cf. chivalric imagery I 763 etc. Devils' feats fantastic as
cloud-pictures.   **539 Typhœan** pron. tifían. Apart from his character
as anti-Zeus monster (I 199) Typhoeus' name meant whirlwind. The
devils continue to be shown in terms of meteorological disaster; they were
thought to inhabit the element of air especially. They had hurled hills in
heaven VI 639. **fell !**   **541** as many stresses in this line as you like.
542 Alcídès Hercules. On his way home from a conquest in Oechalia
(oykarlia) he sent ahead for a robe in which to make a thank-offering to
Zeus. His wife sent him one dipped in a love-potion to make him faithful
to her; but it was poisonous and when he put it on it stuck to his skin.
Mad with pain, he threw Lichas, the messenger who brought the robe,
into the sea from the top of a cliff in Euboea; then (M varies the usual
account) climbed Mt Oeta (oyta) in Thessaly, tore up trees to make a
pyre and was burnt on it. See Ovid *Met.* IX Sophocles *Trachiniae*. More
chaotic behaviour, opposite to Orphic charm. Tense awkward rhythms
imply frustration; it is largely sexual – the aphrodisiac, the phallic
pines – as Satan admits IV 509. Robe also image of inescapable selfhood.
547 retreated withdrawn, dropped out. Language romantic, archaic.
The aesthetes of hell sing plaintively about themselves and how hard done

With notes angelical to many a harp
Their own heroic deeds and hapless fall
By doom of battle; and complain that fate   550
Free virtue should enthral to force or chance.
Their song was partial, but the harmony
(What could it less when spirits immortal sing?)
Suspended hell, and took with ravishment
The thronging audience. In discóurse more sweet   555
(For eloquence the soul, song charms the sense)
Others apart sat on a hill retired,
In thoughts more elevate, and reasoned high
Of providence, foreknowledge, will, and fate,
Fixed fate, free will, foreknowledge absolute,   560
And found no end, in wandering mazes lost.
Of good and evil much they argued then,
Of happiness and final misery,
Passion and apathy, and glory and shame,
Vain wisdom all, and false philosophy: 565
Yet with a pleasing sorcery could charm
Pain for a while or anguish, and excite
Fallacious hope, or arm the obdurèd breast
With stubborn patience as with triple steel.

    Another part in squadrons and gross bands,   570
On bold adventure to discover wide
That dismal world, if any clime perhaps
Might yield them easier habitation, bend
Four ways their flying march, along the banks
Of four infernal rivers that disgorge   575
Into the burning lake their baleful streams;

by they are, in the usual devils' terms of fate and chance.   **551 virtue**
strength. They claim they were totally free agents in the universe; hence
their song is prejudiced.   **554 Suspended** held rapt. A parody of
Orpheus, whose song intermitted all pain when he went to hades to fetch
back his wife.   **559 providence**... parody of theological discussion.
God discusses these doctrines III 96 and M *passim* in *De doctrina*; the
point seems to be that the devils' intellectuality is frivolous because they
exercise it for entertainment, without beliefs or aims; as unfallen angels
they would have discoursed intuitively anyway v 498.   **564 Passion
and apathy** emotion and non-emotion. Refers to stoicism: see intro.
570 gross tightknit.

Abhorrèd Styx the flood of deadly hate,
Sad Acheron of sorrow, black and deep;
Cocytus, named of lamentation loud
Heard on the rueful stream; fierce Phlegethon   580
Whose waves of torrent fire inflame with rage.
Far off from these a slow and silent stream,
Lethè the river of oblivion rolls
Her watery labyrinth, whereof who drinks,
Forthwith his former state and being forgets,   585
Forgets both joy and grief, pleasure and pain.
Beyond this flood a frozen continent
Lies dark and wild, beat with perpetual storms
Of whirlwind and dire hail, which on firm land
Thaws not, but gathers heap, and ruin seems   590
Of ancient pile; all else deep snow and ice,
A gulf profound as that Serbonian bog
Betwixt Damiata and Mount Casius old,
Where armies whole have sunk: the parching air
Burns frore, and cold performs the effect of fire.   595
Thither by harpy-footed Furies haled,
At certain revolutions all the damned
Are brought: and feel by turns the bitter change
Of fierce extremes, extremes by change more fierce,

577 **Styx** the rivers come from *Aeneid* VI, *Inferno* xiv, the lake *Revelation* xix; they parallel the 4 rivers of Eden IV 233 and the living waters of heaven. M explains the emotions that their Greek names stand for.   583 **Lethe** river in the classical underworld and Dante's *Purgatorio*. When souls of the dead drank of it they forgot their earthly lives; but the devils, though they had been briefly concussed by the burning lake, can't get the permanent oblivion of Lethe 604.   587 **flood** river.   590 **ruin** piled-up hail looks like the ruin of an old building. Ice as well as fire a traditional feature of hell but this description comes from reports of 16c polar explorers.   592 **Serbonian bog** dried-up lake in Nile delta between Damietta and a huge dune called Mt Casius. When sand blew into the lake it looked like solid desert; part of a Persian army marched in and sank. Typhon fell in too. Sand = hot ice? both sterile, treacherous.   594 **parching** withering, with heat or cold. 595 **frore** freezing; archaic.   596 **Furies** avenging goddesses; personified the curses on a criminal; pursued evildoers as in Aeschylus *Eumenides*, Eliot *Family reunion*. Harpies were female monsters with wings who carried people off and tortured them with their talons. Rather dragged-in here?   597 **revolutions** seasons. M uses present tense now – hell a general concept rather than in the plot.   599 **extremes** rhetorical

From beds of raging fire to starve in ice   600
Their soft ethereal warmth, and there to pine
Immovable, infixed, and frozen round,
Periods of time, thence hurried back to fire.
They ferry over this Lethéan sound
Both to and fro, their sorrow to augment,   605
And wish and struggle, as they pass, to reach
The tempting stream, with one small drop to lose
In sweet forgetfulness all pain and woe,
All in one moment, and so near the brink;
But fate withstands, and to oppose the attempt   610
Medusa with Gorgonian terror guards'
The ford, and of itself the water flies
All taste of living wight, as once it fled
The lip of Tantalus. Thus roving on
In cónfused march forlorn, the adventurous bands   615
With shuddering horror pale, and eyes aghast
Viewed first their lámentable lot, and found
No rest: through many a dark and dreary vale
They passed, and many a region dolorous,
O'er many a frozen, many a fiery alp,   620
Rocks, caves, lakes, fens, bogs, dens, and shades of death,
A universe of death, which God by curse
Created evil, for evil only good,
Where all life dies, death lives, and nature breeds,
Perverse, all monstrous, all prodigious things,   625

figure of antimetabole, reversed repetition; rather old-fashioned; cf. 624.
600 starve perish: Anglo-Saxon *steorfan* to die, especially of cold or
hunger. Torturers still do this.   **604 sound** estuary.   **610 fate
withstands** it is prohibited by the nature of things.   **611 Medusa** most
famous of the three Gorgons. They were monstrous women with wings,
brazen claws, snakes for hair and huge teeth. Medusa had once been
beautiful but she became so ugly that anyone who looked at her face was
turned to stone (see myth of Perseus). Perhaps part of a train of ideas:
Stoic stubbornness...ice...stone.   **614 Tantalus** punished in hades
by raging thirst while bound in a lake whose waters receded whenever he
tried to drink.   **615 forlorn** lost. M repeats this motif at VII 20, X 920.
adventurous exploring, voyaging (not bold).   **625 prodigious** unnatural. This is the opposite of the universe. Everything that exists was
created by God, so he must have created hell; but this is not a theme that

Abominable, inutterable, and worse
Than fables yet have feigned, or fear conceived,
Gorgons and Hydras, and Chimeras dire.

    Mean while the adversary of God and man,
Satan with thoughts inflamed of highest design,   630
Puts on swift wings, and towards the gates of hell
Explores his solitary flight; sometimes
He scours the right hand coast, sometimes the left,
Now shaves with level wing the deep, then soars
Up to the fiery concave towering high.   635
As when far off at sea a fleet descried
Hangs in the clouds, by equinoctial winds
Close sailing from Bengala, or the isles
Of Ternate and Tidore, whence merchants bring
Their spicy drugs: they on the trading flood   640
Through the wide Ethiopian to the Cape
Ply stemming nightly toward the pole. So seemed
Far off the flying fiend: at last appear
Hell bounds high reaching to the horrid roof,
And thrice threefold the gates; three folds were brass, 645
Three irön, three of adamántine rock,
Impenetrable, impaled with circling fire,
Yet unconsumed. Before the gates there sat
On either side a formidable shape;
The one seemed woman to the waist, and fair,   650
But ended foul in many a scaly fold

theologians or editors dwell on.   **628 Hydras** the Hydra was a colossal
snake with 9 heads; the Chimera a female monster with 3 heads, and
body composed of lion, goat, dragon; it stands for illusion, fantasy.
629 adversary literal meaning of *satan*.   **630 design** intention, ambition.   **631 Puts on** poetic idiom for flies fast.   **632 explores** tries out.
637 clouds it is a mirage. Continues oriental, voyaging and weather
motifs. The East Indiamen are sailing southwards from Bengal or two of
the Spice Islands, close-hauled to the trade wind which blows across the
Indian Ocean at the equinoxes (or in the tropics; not sure). A modern
scene for M yet romantic, and also close to Satan, bringing a spicy drug
to Eve.   **647 impaled** fenced.   **650 fair** beautiful.   **651 fold** twist,
coil; often used of snake and dragon tails.

Voluminous and vast, a serpent armed
With mortal sting: about her middle round
A cry of hell hounds never ceasing barked
With wide Cerbérean mouths full loud, and rung   655
A hideous peal: yet, when they list, would creep,
If aught disturbed their noise, into her womb,
And kennel there, yet there still barked and howled
Within unseen. Far less abhorred than these
Vexed Scylla bathing in the sea that parts   660
Calabria from the hoarse Trinacrian shore:
Nor uglier follow the night-hag, when called
In secret, riding through the air she comes
Lured with the smell of infant blood, to dance
With Lapland witches, while the labouring moon   665
Eclipses at their charms. The other shape,
If shape it might be called that shape had none
Distinguishable in member, joint, or limb,
Or substance might be called that shadow seemed,
For each seemed either; black it stood as night,   670
Fierce as ten Furies, terrible as hell,
And shook a dreadful dart; what seemed his head
The likeness of a kingly crown had on.
Satan was now at hand, and from his seat
The monster moving onwards came as fast   675
With horrid strides, hell trembled as he strode.
The undaunted fiend what this might be admired,

652 Voluminous coiled like a scroll (Lat. *volumen*). Unparaphrasable
description.   **653 sting** symbolic: sin brings death; 'the sting of death is
sin' *I Corinthians* xv. **round** round about her middle.   **654 cry** pack.
655 Cerberean Cerberus was the many-headed dog who guarded hades.
660 Scylla bathed in a rock-pool that Circe, who was jealous of her, had
bewitched. The water made dogs grow out of her pudenda and replace
body and legs from the waist down. Later she was turned into a rock in the
dangerous straits between Calabria (in Italy) and Sicily. Syntax: Sin's dogs
more abhorrent than those that afflicted Scylla.   **662 night-hag** Hecate,
triform goddess of witchcraft, the moon, the dead. Portress of hades.
She helped Circe bewitch Scylla's pool. Here the witches of Lapland,
traditional centre of the cult, have conjured her up by sacrificing a baby
(witches were blamed for infant mortality); she is followed by her own
train of flying hellhounds.   **665 labouring** disturbed.   **671 Furies**
see 596.   **672 dart** javelin.   **677 admired** wondered. Kind of rhyme.

Admired, not feared; God and his Son except,
Created thing nought valued he nor shunned;
And with disdainful look thus first began.   680

Whence and what art thou, éxecrable shape,
That dar'st, though grim and terrible, advance
Thy miscreated front athwart my way
To yonder gates? through them I mean to pass,
That be assured, without leave asked of thee: 685
Retire, or taste thy folly, and learn by proof,
Hell-born, not to contend with spirits of heaven.

To whom the goblin full of wrath replied,
Art thou that traitor angel, art thou he,
Who first broke peace in heaven and faith, till then 690
Unbroken, and in proud rebellious arms
Drew after him the third part of heaven's sons
Conjúred against the Highest, for which both thou
And they outcast from God, are here condemned
To waste eternal days in woe and pain?   695
And reckon'st thou thyself with spirits of heaven,
Hell-doomed, and breath'st defiance here and scorn
Where I reign king, and to enrage thee more,
Thy king and lord? Back to thy punishment,
False fugitive, and to thy speed add wings,   700
Lest with a whip of scorpions I pursue
Thy lingering, or with one stroke of this dart
Strange horror seize thee, and pangs unfelt before.

So spake the grisly terror, and in shape,
So speaking and so threatening, grew tenfold   705
More dreadful and deform: on the other side
Incensed with indignation Satan stood

693 conjured sworn to conspire.   **696 reckon'st** do you count yourself
a spirit of heaven?   **697 Hell-doomed** retort to Satan's hellborn.
702 one stroke of stress all three syllables?   **704 grisly terror** cf. meagre
shadow, grim feature x 264–79.   **705 So...so** while. **grew tenfold
More** stress all four?

Unterrified, and like a comet burned,
That fires the length of Ophiúcus huge
In the arctic sky, and from his horrid hair   710
Shakes pestilence and war. Each at the head
Levelled his deadly aim; their fatal hands
No second stroke intend, and such a frown
Each cast at the other, as when two black clouds
With heaven's artillery fraught, come rattling on   715
Over the Caspian, then stand front to front
Hovering a space, till winds the signal blow
To join their dark encounter in mid air:
So frowned the mighty combatants, that hell
Grew darker at their frown, so matched they stood;   720
For never but once more was either like
To meet so great a foe: and now great deeds
Had been achieved, whereof all hell had rung,
Had not the snaky sorceress that sat
Fast by hell gate, and kept the fatal key,   725
Risen, and with hideous outcry rushed between.

O father, what intends thy hand, she cried,
Against thy only son? What fury, O son,
Possesses thee to bend that mortal dart
Against thy father's head? and know'st for whom?   730
For him who sits above and laughs the while
At thee ordained his drudge, to execute
Whate'er his wrath, which he calls justice, bids,
His wrath which one day will destroy ye both.

709 Ophiucus the Serpent-bearer, a large constellation in the northern
hemisphere. M probably means a comet which appeared in 1618; Evelyn
claims in his diary to remember hearing talk about it when he was four; it
was taken to have caused the Thirty Years War.   **710 horrid hair** the
comet's bristling tail.   **716 Caspian** notoriously stormy. The simile takes
a double loop into narrative with So . . . so: they frowned as darkly as those
clouds, and they were as evenly matched.   **721 like** likely. Referring to
Christ who was to harrow hell, and finally destroy Death x 633 and Satan
XII 453.   **725 key** not mentioned before. Symbolism ?   **729 bend** aim.
730 know'st you know whom it would please if you killed your father:
God.

She spake, and at her words the hellish pest   735
Forbore, then these to her Satan returned:

So strange thy outcry, and thy words so strange
Thou interposest, that my sudden hand
Prevented spares to tell thee yet by deeds
What it intends; till first I know of thee,   740
What thing thou art, thus double-formed, and why
In this infernal vale first met thou call'st
Me father, and that phantasm call'st my son?
I know thee not, nor ever saw till now
Sight more detestable than him and thee.   745

To whom thus the portress of hell gate replied:
Hast thou forgot me then, and do I seem
Now in thine eye so foul, once deemed so fair
In heaven, when at the assembly, and in sight
Of all the seraphim with thee combined   750
In bold conspiracy against heaven's King,
All on a sudden miserable pain
Surprised thee, dim thine eyes, and dizzy swum
In darkness, while thy head flames thick and fast
Threw forth, till on the left side opening wide,   755
Likest to thee in shape and countenance bright,
Then shining heavenly fair, a goddess armed
Out of thy head I sprung: amazement seized
All the host of heaven; back they recoiled afraid
At first, and called me Sin, and for a sign   760
Portentous held me; but familiar grown,
I pleased, and with attractive graces won
The most averse, thee chiefly, who full oft
Thyself in me thy perfect image viewing

735 pest plague.   **736 these** words.   **739 spares** my hand, held
back, refrains.   **742 first met** the first time we have ever met, yet you
call me father.   **746 To whom** elided to toom.   **749 assembly**
there is no mention of it in the rebellion story v.   **755 left side** parody
of Eve issuing from Adam's rib; blood from Christ's side; Athena from
head of Zeus. The basis is the pun in conception=idea, and=procrea-
tion.   **757 Then shining** Satan was still bright then. **armed** in armour.
760 sign pun on sin but no connection really.   **764 The line parodies**

Becam'st enamoured, and such joy thou took'st   765
With me in secret, that my womb conceived
A growing burden. Meanwhile war arose,
And fields were fought in heaven; wherein remained
(For what could else) to our almighty Foe
Clear victory, to our part loss and rout   770
Through all the empyrean: down they fell
Driven headlong from the pitch of heaven, down
Into this deep, and in the general fall
I also; at which time this powerful key
Into my hand was given, with charge to keep   775
These gates for ever shut, which none can pass
Without my opening. Pensive here I sat
Alone, but long I sat not, till my womb
Pregnant by thee, and now excessive grown
Prodigious motion felt and rueful throes.   780
At last this odious offspring whom thou seest
Thine own begotten, breaking violent way
Tore through my entrails, that with fear and pain
Distorted, all my nether shape thus grew
Transformed: but he my inbred enemy   785
Forth issued, brandishing his fatal dart
Made to destroy: I fled, and cried out Death;
Hell trembled at the hideous name, and sighed
From all her caves, and back resounded Death.
I fled, but he pursued (though more, it seems,   790
Inflamed with lust than rage) and swifter far,
Me overtook his mother all dismayed,
And in embraces forcible and foul
Ingendering with me, of that rape begot
These yelling monsters that with ceaseless cry   795

Son as mirror of Father v 716, man as image of God, Eve mirror of Adam;
and myth of Narcissus.   **772 pitch** height.   **779 excessive** ready to
extrude its contents (early 17c use).   **780 motion** contractions in
labour. Usually reserved for defecating; this passage repeats anal motif
of I.   **784 nether shape** the birth of Death turned her into snakes from
the waist down.   **787 Death** she cried this thinking she was going
to be killed, not knowing yet that it was Death himself chasing her.
792 Distorted syntax mimes confusion of incestuous rape.

Surround me, as thou saw'st, hourly conceived
And hourly born, with sorrow infinite
To me, for when they list into the womb
That bred them they return, and howl and gnaw
My bowels, their repast; then bursting forth   800
Afresh with conscious terrors vex me round,
That rest or intermission none I find.
Before mine eyes in opposition sits
Grim Death my son and foe, who sets them on,
And me his parent would full soon devour   805
For want of other prey, but that he knows
His end with mine involved; and knows that I
Should prove a bitter morsel, and his bane,
Whenever that shall be; so fate pronounced.
But thou, O father, I forewarn thee, shun   810
His deadly arrow; neither vainly hope
To be invulnerable in those bright arms,
Though tempered heavenly, for that mortal dint,
Save he who reigns above, none can resist.

  She finished, and the subtle fiend his lore   815
Soon learned, now milder, and thus answered smooth.
Dear daughter, since thou claim'st me for thy sire,
And my fair son here show'st me, the dear pledge
Of dalliance had with thee in heaven, and joys
Then sweet, now sad to mention, through dire change   820
Befallen us unforeseen, unthought of, know
I come no enemy, but to set free
From out this dark and dismal house of pain,
Both him and thee, and all the heavenly host
Of spirits that in our just pretences armed   825
Fell with us from on high: from them I go

798 Repeats 656. May hint at Jezebel, emblem of idolatry and whoring,
whose corpse was eaten by dogs *II Kings* ix.   **801 conscious terrors**
apprehension; or possibly pangs of conscience (not sure).   **813 dint**
blow.   **814 Save** except.   **815 subtle** clever. **lore** lesson.   **818 pledge
of dalliance** token of lovemaking. Tone friendly, mildly romantic.
821 unthought of unexpected.   **825 pretences** claims.

This uncouth errand sole, and one for all
Myself expose, with lonely steps to tread
The unfounded deep, and through the void immense
To search with wandering quest a place foretold   830
Should be, and, by concurring signs, ere now
Created vast and round, a place of bliss
In the purlieus of heaven, and therein placed
A race of upstart creatures, to supply
Perhaps our vacant room, though more removed,   835
Lest heaven surcharged with potent multitude
Might hap to move new broils: be this or aught
Than this more secret now designed, I haste
To know, and this once known, shall soon return,
And bring ye to the place where thou and Death   840
Shall dwell at ease, and up and down unseen
Wing silently the buxom air, embalmed
With odours; there ye shall be fed and filled
Immeasurably, all things shall be your prey.
    He ceased, for both seemed highly pleased,   845
       and Death
Grinned horrible a ghastly smile, to hear
His famine should be filled, and blessed his maw
Destined to that good hour: no less rejoiced
His mother bad, and thus bespake her sire.

    The key of this infernal pit by due,   850

829 unfounded bottomless, uncreated and shapeless.   **830 foretold** a place it was foretold would come into being and which, to judge by signs that point that way too, has already been created. We don't know what the signs are. Syntax continues compressed.   **834 supply** fill up.   **835 more removed** further away.   **836 surcharged** overfilled. In case the overpopulation of heaven might start another war. Flippant speculation; the whole speech boring and repetitive.   **837 be this** whether this is so, or something more secret is now planned...   **839 return** he does x 397, and they invade earth.   **842 buxom** pliant. They will enjoy earth's air instead of hell's smoke; and the air, or they, will be fragrant with perfume instead of sulphur; but embalmed, though it means perfumed, reminds us that they are creatures of corruption.   **848 Destined** devoted.   **849 bespake** said to.   **850 due** right of possession; or duty.

And by command of heaven's all-powerful King
I keep, by him forbidden to unlock
These adamantine gates; against all force
Death ready stands to interpose his dart,
Fearless to be o'ermatched by living might.   855
But what owe I to his commands above
Who hates me, and hath hither thrust me down
Into this gloom of Tartarus profound,
To sit in hateful office here confined,
Inhabitant of heaven, and heavenly-born,   860
Here in perpetual agony and pain,
With terrors and with clamours compassed round
Of mine own brood, that on my bowels feed?
Thou art my father, thou my author, thou
My being gav'st me; whom should I obey   865
But thee, whom follow? thou wilt bring me soon
To that new world of light and bliss, among
The gods who live at ease, where I shall reign
At thy right hand voluptuous, as beseems
Thy daughter and thy darling, without end.   870

    Thus saying, from her side the fatal key,
Sad instrument of all our woe, she took;
And towards the gate rolling her bestial train,
Forthwith the huge portcullis high updrew,
Which but herself not all the Stygian powers   875
Could once have moved; then in the key-hole turns
The intricate wards, and every bolt and bar
Of massy iron or solid rock with ease
Unfastens: on a sudden open fly
With impetuous recoil and jarring sound   880
The infernal doors, and on their hinges grate
Harsh thunder, that the lowest bottom shook

859 office duty.   **869 right hand** parodies Christ.   **872 all our woe**
from I 3.   **875 but** except for.

Of Érèbus. She opened, but to shut
Excelled her power; the gates wide open stood,
That with extended wings a bannered host   885
Under spread ensigns marching might pass through
With horse and chariots ranked in loose array;
So wide they stood, and like a furnace mouth
Cast forth redounding smoke and ruddy flame.
Before their eyes in sudden view appear   890
The secrets of the hoary deep, a dark
Illimitable ocean without bound,
Without dimension, where length, breadth, and highth,
And time and place are lost; where eldest Night
And Chaos, ancestors of Nature, hold   895
Eternal anarchy, amidst the noise
Of endless wars, and by confusion stand.
For hot, cold, moist, and dry, four champions fierce
Strive here for maistrie, and to battle bring
Their embryon atoms; they around the flag   900
Of each his faction, in their several clans,
Light-armed or heavy, sharp, smooth, swift or slow,
Swarm populous, unnumbered as the sands
Of Barca or Cyrénè's torrid soil,
Levied to side with warring winds, and poise   905
Their lighter wings. To whom these most adhere,
He rules a moment; Chaos umpire sits,

883 **Erebus** vestibule of hades. Cf. opening of heaven gate to create world VII 205. Satan wants to welcome Adam and Eve through hellgates IV 381. 889 **redounding** surging. 891 **secrets** secret places. **hoary** grey or mouldy with age. 895 **ancestors** in some cosmogonies, including Hesiod's and a hint in *Genesis* i 2, principles of non-entity like chaos and darkness produce light, water etc. before first gods appear. 896 **anarchy** with no ruler (Greek *archos* ruler); used parallel to monarchy etc. 898 **champions** protagonists – old-fashioned, cf. maistrie. The quality of each element fights for itself instead of combining to form matter. Potential atoms fly about like a sandstorm instead of settling to form the elements listed in 912. See intro. Levied=literally raised, as well as enlisted (verbal playfulness chaotic or ingenious?). It's unclear whether 'poise their lighter wings' is inside the simile: if so, it means the sand is raised to give weight to the winds; if outside, the atoms gathered round an element hover there, lighter than grains of sand. Barca and Cyrene towns in Libya well-known in classical history.

And by decision more embroils the fray
By which he reigns: next him high arbiter
Chance governs all. Into this wild abyss,   910
The womb of Nature and perhaps her grave,
Of neither sea, nor shore, nor air, nor fire,
But all these in their pregnant causes mixed
Confusedly, and which thus must ever fight,
Unless the almighty Maker them ordain   915
His dark materials to create more worlds,
Into this wild abyss the wary fiend
Stood on the brink of hell and looked a while,
Pondering his voyage; for no narrow frith
He had to cross. Nor was his ear less pealed   920
With noises loud and ruinous (to compare
Great things with small) than when Bellona storms,
With all her battering engines bent to rase
Some capital city; or less than if this frame
Of heaven were falling, and these elements   925
In mutiny had from her axle torn
The steadfast earth. At last his sail-broad vans
He spreads for flight, and in the surging smoke
Uplifted spurns the ground, thence many a league
As in a cloudy chair ascending rides   930
Audacious, but that seat soon failing, meets
A vast vacuity: all unawares
Fluttering his pennons vain plumb down he drops

911 grave some thought the universe would revert to chaos after the end of
the world. According to some 20c cosmological theories it will then expand
into creation again.   **913 pregnant causes** embryonic matter. In
Aristotelian philosophy everything had 4 'causes': material=its matter,
as here; efficient=agency producing it; formal=form, essence, what it
'is'; final=purpose, end, what it will become.   **915 ordain** put in
order.   **917** Catches up 910 as if after taking breath; cf. insertion of
'Stood...hell' before the looks; and l 300–14.   **919 frith** firth, strait.
920 pealed made to ring.   **922 Bellona** goddess of war. The negative
nexus, and apology for scale, conventional in epic simile.   **924 this frame**
the fabric of our sky. Axle is the poles.   **927 vans** wings.   **930 chair**
a puff of thick smoke lifts him, then drops away as in an air-pocket
where his wings (pennons) can't support him. The chair suggests masque
machinery, like the levitation scene of pantomime. Slapstick.

Ten thousand fathom deep, and to this hour
Down had been falling, had not by ill chance   935
The strong rebuff of some tumultuous cloud
Instínct with fire and nitre hurried him
As many miles aloft: that fury stayed,
Quenched in a boggy Syrtis, neither sea,
Nor good dry land: nigh foundered on he fares,   940
Treading the crude consistence, half on foot,
Half flying; behoves him now both oar and sail.
As when a gryphon through the wilderness
With wingèd course o'cr hill or moory dale,
Pursues the Arimaspian, who by stealth   945
Had from his wakeful custody purloined
The guarded gold: so eagerly the fiend
O'er bog or steep, through straight, rough, dense, or rare,
With head, hands, wings, or feet pursues his way,
And swims or sinks, or wades, or creeps, or flies.   950
   At length a universal hubbub wild
Of stunning sounds and voices all confused
Borne through the hollow dark assaults his ear
With loudest vehemence: thither he plies,
Undaunted to meet there whatever power   955
Or spirit of the nethermost abyss
Might in that noise reside, of whom to ask
Which way the nearest coast of darkness lies
Bordering on light; when straight behold the throne
Of Chaos, and his dark pavilion spread   960
Wide on the wasteful deep; with him enthroned
Sat sable-vested Night, eldest of things,

935 Note stresses, and hads.   **937 instínct** propelled by natural
gunpowder. It blows him up again, till the explosion is damped in an
area like the great quicksands of Syrtis near Tripoli.   **941 crude** raw.
943 gryphon or griffin, fabulous eagle-lion which guarded goldmines
in Siberia against the Arimaspi, people who lived nearby. Gold often
guarded by monsters in myth; actual mines in Urals. Moory=marshy.
948 straight level.   **951 hubbub** from Irish in 16c. Word upon word.
957 noise treated as a place.   **959 straight** suddenly.   **960 pavilion**
royal encampment. Used of God *Psalm* xviii.   **961 wasteful** desolate;
limitless; sterile – all 3 meanings.   **962 sable-vested** black-clad.

The consort of his reign; and by them stood
Orcus and Adès, and the dreaded name
Of Demogorgon; Rumour next and Chance,   965
And Tumult and Confusion all embroiled,
And Discord with a thousand various mouths.

To whom Satan turning boldly, thus. Ye powers
And spirits of this nethermost abyss,
Chaos and ancient Night, I come no spy,   970
With purpose to explore or to disturb
The secrets of your realm, but by constraint
Wandering this darksome desert, as my way
Lies through your spacious empire up to light,
Alone, and without guide, half lost, I seek   975
What readiest path leads where your gloomy bounds
Confine with heaven; or if some other place
From your dominion won, the ethereal King
Possesses lately, thither to arrive
I travel this profound, direct my course;   980
Directed no mean recompense it brings
To your behoof, if I that region lost,
All usurpation thence expelled, reduce
To her original darkness and your sway
(Which is my present journey) and once more   985
Erect the standard there of ancient Night.
Yours be the advantage all, mine the revenge.

Thus Satan; and him thus the anarch old
With faltering speech and visage incomposed

964 Orcus Pluto or Dis, god of hades; also called (H)ades. 'The shadowy
flowers of Orcus remember thee' Pound *Doria*. Demogorgon is another
primordial force and/or underworld god, never fully defined. 'Dreaded
name of D' is a Latin way of saying 'D his very self'. In renaissance art it
was acceptable to have personifications like Tumult inhabiting tumult.
977 confine border.   **980 profound** used as noun. He is asking
directions to the new-created world. If they direct his way, it will bring
them reward to their benefit, if he, having expelled the usurping creatures
from that world now lost to them, turn it back into chaos, which is the
purpose of his journey.   **988 anarch** Chaos.

Answered. I know thee, stranger, who thou art,   990
That mighty leading angel, who of late
Made head against heaven's King, though overthrown.
I saw and heard, for such a numerous host
Fled not in silence through the frighted deep
With ruin upon ruin, rout on rout,   995
Confusion worse confounded; and heaven gates
Poured out by millions her victorious bands
Pursuing. I upon my frontiers here
Keep residence; if all I can will serve,
That little which is left so to defend,   1000
Encroached on still through our intestine broils
Weakening the sceptre of old Night: first hell
Your dungeon stretching far and wide beneath;
Now lately heaven and earth, another world
Hung o'er my realm, linked in a golden chain   1005
To that side heaven from whence your legions fell:
If that way be your walk, you have not far;
So much the nearer danger; go and speed;
Havoc and spoil and ruin are my gain.

He ceased; and Satan stayed not to reply,   1010
But glad that now his sea should find a shore,
With fresh alacrity and force renewed
Springs upward like a pyramid of fire
Into the wild expanse, and through the shock
Of fighting elements, on all sides round   1015
Environed wins his way; harder beset
And more endangered, than when Argo passed

999 if all I can... if the most I can do will help – staying here to defend what little is left. He seems not to complete his sentences. **1001 intestine broils** civil wars. **1004 world** universe with earth at the centre, conglobed by heavenly spheres. **1007** Very colloquial, and doddering. Satan's account of this conversation at x 477 is quite different. **1013 pyramid** flamy spire. **1017 Argo** ship in which Jason and the Argonauts sailed to capture the golden fleece from the Crimea. They had to pass through the Bosphorus where floating islands nearly crushed them but a dove piloted them between. Ulysses had to steer to port, towards the rock Charybdis, to avoid the rock Scylla (cf. 660); both rocks had whirlpools below.

Through Bosphorus, betwixt the justling rocks:
Or when Ulýsses on the larboard shunned
Charybdis, and by the other whirlpool steered.   1020
So he with difficulty and labour hard
Moved on, with difficulty and labour he;
But he once past, soon after when man fell,
Strange alteration! Sin and Death amain
Following his track, such was the will of heaven,   1025
Paved after him a broad and beaten way
Over the dark abyss, whose boiling gulf
Tamely endured a bridge of wondrous length
From hell continued reaching the utmost orb
Of this frail world; by which the spirits perverse   1030
With easy intercourse pass to and fro
To tempt or punish mortals, except whom
God and good angels guard by special grace.
But now at last the sacred influence
Of light appears, and from the walls of heaven   1035
Shoots far into the bosom of dim night
A glimmering dawn; here nature first begins
Her farthest verge, and chaos to retire
As from her outmost works a broken foe
With tumult less and with less hostile din,   1040
That Satan with less toil, and now with ease
Wafts on the calmer wave by dubious light
And like a weather-beaten vessel holds
Gladly the port, though shrouds and tackle torn;
Or in the emptier waste, resembling air,   1045
Weighs his spread wings, at leisure to behold
Far off the empyreal heaven, extended wide

1022 Elaborate iteration mimes difficulty and leads to stress on final *he*;
but after him Sin and Death easily paved the way between hell and earth
x 293.   **1029 utmost orb** outermost sphere.   **1033** Hard to accept
all the *g*'s.   **1034 influence** actual effect, as of sunlight, cf. III 586,
IV 671; sacred because emanating from God: see III 1.   **1037 nature**
created universe; chaos retreats defeated from the outermost fortifica-
tions/creations of nature.   **1040 less** one of several devices used here
to close down hell, end the Book, lighten tone.   **1043 holds** makes for.
1045 emptier than chaos was.   **1046 weighs** rests on.   **1047 heaven**

In circuit, undetermined square or round,
With opal towers and battlements adorned
Of living sapphire, once his native seat;   1050
And fast by hanging in a golden chain
This pendent world, in bigness as a star
Of smallest magnitude close by the moon.
Thither full fraught with mischievous revenge,
Accursed, and in a cursèd hour he hies.   1055

so large S can't determine whether straight or curved. Jewels from
Revelation xxi. Empyreal = made of fire because that was the purest
element; the word means pure, bright, celestial.   **1051 chain** emblem
of moral bond; faint image of jewellery. Simile says universe : heaven ::
tiny star : moon.

Appendix to Book I

The introduction at the beginning of this volume is on the whole aimed at *PL*; and it is discursive. This appendix follows the same order as the introduction; but it simply proposes topics, and offers a few materials. The topics are mostly ones which the poem offers beyond itself.

Invocation

Beginnings

In the introduction we considered the invocation as a part of the epic tradition, and a part of *PL*. We can also consider it as a particular case of a beginning. We can go on to consider beginnings in general. In some cases this will be best done physically, by improvisation or mime or drama; or in some non-verbal expression such as painting or dancing. In this case you probably won't get much further physically than to discover that to begin involves tensing a muscle. If you stay at the verbal level, consider how a particular novel begins; or write a detailed account of how the class or conversation or other circumstance in which this subject is being dealt with did in fact begin.

Muses

Milton's invocation of a muse raises these more general topics: mythology of the muses; Apollonian inspiration versus Dionysiac; the nature of inspiration; patrons, patronesses – why are muses female? who do poets write for? Here are some suggestions and a few materials.

See a dictionary of Greek mythology; Poussin *Parnassus* and *Inspiration of the poet*; Raphael *Parnassus* (with Dante and other renaissance poets assembled with classical gods and poets); Mantegna *Parnassus* (for the muses); Tintoretto *The nine muses*. For a near-contemporary sense of the power of music and the muses, which Milton might have heard, listen to Monteverdi's opera *Orfeo* (1607), especially Act III where Orpheus charms

Charon in hades. Then listen to Holst's *Planets*, and Stravinsky's ballets *Apollo Musagetes* and *Orpheus*; and read Crashaw's poem *Music's duel* (1648).

The muses were related to Dionysus, god of wine, divine madness, ecstasy; but they were especially under the leadership of his 'cool' complement Apollo – god of poetry, prophecy, music, learning. They were originally watersprites: 'Begin then, Sisters of the sacred well...Begin' Milton says in *Lycidas*.

It was during Elizabeth I's reign that poets applied most elaborately to the muses; and tended to conflate them with their patrons or, especially, patronesses (cf. *PL* IX 21). This might be because it was a time when poets wanted to imitate past models; or it might be more indicative of the economics of art, and the artist's position in society.

There was a muse for each art and each genre. Here two of them lament in Spenser's *Tears of the Muses* (part of his *Complaints*, i.e. satires, 1591):

Calliope [muse of epic poetry]
> ...Therefore the nurse of virtue I am hight,
> And golden trumpet of eternity,
> That lowly thoughts lift up to heaven's height
> And mortal men have power to deify;
> Bacchus and Hercules I raised to heaven
> And Charlemagne among the starris seven.
>
> But now will I my golden clarion rend
> And will henceforth immortalise no more:
> Sith I no more find worthy to commend
> For prize of value or for learned lore;
> For noble peers whom I was wont to raise
> Now only seek for pleasure, nought for praise.
>
> Their great revénue all in sumptuous pride
> They spend, that nought to learning they may spare;
> And the rich fee which poets wont divide
> Now parasites and sychophants do share;
> Therefore I mourn and endless sorrow make
> Both for myself and for my sisters' sake...

Urania [muse of divine poetry]
> ...Through knowledge we behold the world's creatiòn,
> How in his cradle first he fostered was;
> And judge of Nature's cunning operatiòn,
> How things she formèd of a formless mass;
> By knowledge we do learn ourselves to know
> And what to man and what to God we owe.
>
> From hence we mount aloft unto the sky
> And look into the crystal firmament;

There we behold the heavens' great hierarchy,
The stars' pure light, the spheres' swift movëment,
The spirits and intelligences fair,
And angels waiting on the Almighty's chair.

The muses were daughters of Zeus and Mnemosyne, goddess of memory. Blake attacked them as representatives of authority and history, as opposed to free invention, in the preface to his poem *Milton* (1804–8). It is his version of Milton's own rejection of classical values; and it is followed, in the lyric usually called *Jerusalem*, by Blake's own version of an invocation:

MILTON

A POEM IN 2 BOOKS

To Justify the Ways of God to Men

PREFACE

The Stolen and Perverted Writings of Homer & Ovid, of Plato & Cicero, which all men ought contemn, are set up by artifice against the Sublime of the Bible; but when the New Age is at leisure to pronounce, all will be set right, & those Grand Works of the more ancient and consciously & professedly Inspired Men will hold their proper rank, & the Daughters of Memory shall become the Daughters of Inspiration. Shakespeare & Milton were both curb'd by the general malady & infection from the silly Greek & Latin slaves of the Sword.

Rouze up, O Young Men of the New Age! set your foreheads against the ignorant Hirelings! For we have Hirelings in the Camp, the Court & the University, who would, if they could, for ever depress Mental and prolong Corporeal War. Painters! on you I call. Sculptors! Architects! Suffer not the fashionable Fools to depress your powers by the prices they pretend to give for contemptible works, or the expensive advertizing boasts that they make of such works; believe Christ & his Apostles that there is a Class of Men whose whole delight is in Destroying. We do not want either Greek or Roman Models if we are but just & true to our own imaginations, those Worlds of Eternity in which we shall live for ever in JESUS OUR LORD.

And did those feet in ancient time [etc]

Holy Spirit

ERNEST JONES from *A psychoanalytic study of the Holy Ghost* 1922 repr. in *Essays in applied psychoanalysis* [International Psychoanalytical Press, London and Vienna] 1923

In the Christian mythology a startling fact appears. It is the only one in which the original figures are no longer present, in which the Trinity to be worshipped no longer consists of the Father, Mother and Son. The Father and Son still appear, but the Mother, the reason for the whole conflict [of primordial incest and parricide proposed by Freud], has been replaced by the mysterious figure of the Holy Ghost...While the sternly patriarchal Hebrew theology, however, banned the Mother to a subordinate part and the Messiah–Son to a remotely distant future, it nevertheless retained the normal relationship of the three. It is probable, therefore, that any elucidation of the change from Mother to Holy Ghost would throw light on the inner nature of the psychological revolution betokened by the development of Judaism into Christianity...The figure thus created represents an androgynic compromise. In surrendering some elements of virility it gains the special female prerogative of child-bearing, and thus combines the advantages of both sexes. The hermaphroditic ideal offered to the world by Christianity had proved of tremendous importance to humanity. We have in it a great reason for the enormous civilising influence of Christianity, since the civilising of primitive man essentially means the mastery of the Oedipus complex and the transformation of much of it into sublimated homosexuality (i.e. herd instinct), without which no social community can exist.

Satan

Literature of Satan

A study of Satan should start with the poetry. What sort of ikons are associated with him by Milton and by other poets? What are the qualities most stressed? How does the verse of his speeches compare with that of the invocations? What are the words he uses of himself? You can rapidly discover what in his own time was special about Milton's Satan by comparing him with Marlowe's Mephistopheles in *Faustus* and Tourneur's Damville in *The atheist's tragedy*. Here are some examples.

HESIOD *Theogony* trans A. S. Way 1934   828 [Zeus defeats Typhoeus]

From all those heads as he savagely glared the fire blazed red.
Voices there were withal in every hideous head
Which uttered all manner of sounds unspeakable...
         ...Earth groaned as in agony-throes.
At the meeting of these fierce heat on the violet sea took hold,
At the thunder and lightning, the flame from the monster's jaws outrolled,
And the scorching winds and the thunderbolts blazing luridly.
Then steamed all earth and heaven, and boiled the depths of the sea:
Maddened the league-long rollers that crashed on the shuddering strand
At the tramp of the charge of the Deathless, and ceaselessly quaked the
    land.

Yea, Hades trembled, the netherworld King of the dead which have died,
And the Titans in Hell's black dens who with ancient Kronos abide,
At the quenchless uproar as the dread strife swayed from side to side.
But when Zeus had upgathered his might, and had grasped his weapons
    in hand,
The thunder, the lightning, the thunderbolt's luridly blazing brand,

From Olympus he leapt on his foe, and struck; and his levin-fire
Consumed and blasted the marvellous heads of the monster dire.
By the scourge of his blows overmastered fell that demon then
A maimed mass crashing down, and huge earth groaned again,
And flames from the levin-blasted lord shot every way
Through the dim dark glens of the rough-scarped mountain where stricken
    he lay.
And of huge earth no small part was burned without and within
By the fervent breath of the flame, and melted even as tin
Is molten by art of men in the smooth-channelled clay, mid the roar
Of the furnace; as iron, the which is of all the stubbornest ore,
Is by the ravening fire subdued mid the glens of a hill,
And melted in moulds of the earth divine by the Fire-god's skill;
So molten was earth in the splendour-glow of blazing fire.
And Zeus into wide Hell hurled him adown in indignant ire.

DANTE from *Inferno* xxxiv

    Come quando una grossa nebbia spira,
      o quando l'emisperio nostro annotta
      par da lungi un molin che il vento gira:

    veder mi parve un tal 'dificio allotta;
      poi per lo vento mi ritrinsi retro
      al duca mio, che non li era altra grotta.

    Già era, e con paura il metto in metro,
      là dove l'ombre eran tutte coperte,
      a trasparean come festuca in vetro.

    Altre sono a giacere, altre stanno erte,
      quella col capo e qualla con le piante;
      altra, com' arco, il volto a' piedi inverte.

    Quando noi fummo fatti tanto avante,
      ch' al mio maestro piacque di mostrarmi
      la creatura ch' ebbe il bel sembiante....

    Lo imperador del doloroso regno
      da mezzo il petto uscìa fuor della ghiaccia;
      e più con un gigante io mi convegno

    che i giganti non fan con le sue braccia:
      vedi oramai quant' esser dee quel tutto
      ch' a così fatte parti si confaccia.

    S'ei fu sì bel com' egli è ora brutto
      e contra il suo Fattore alzò le ciglia,
      ben dee da lui procedere ogni lutto.

    Like, when a thick mist breathes, or our half of the globe darkens, a
windmill looms in the distance: such an edifice did I now seem to see;
and, for the wind, shrank behind my guide, there being no other shelter.
Already I had come (and with fear I put it into verse) where the souls were
encased in ice and shone through like straw behind glass. Some are lying;
some stand upright, this on its head and that upon its soles; another, like
a bow, bends face to feet. When we had proceeded on so far, that it
pleased my guide to show me the creature which was once so fair...

The emperor of the dolorous realm from mid breast stood forth out of the ice; and I in size am liker to a giant than the giants are to his arms: mark how great that whole must be, which corresponds to such a part. If he was once as beautiful as he is ugly now, and lifted up his brows against his Maker, well may all affliction come from him.

P. B. SHELLEY from *A defence of poetry* 1821

The poetry of Dante may be considered as the bridge thrown over the stream of time, which unites the modern and ancient world. The distorted notions of invisible things which Dante and his rival Milton have idealised, are merely the mask and the mantle in which these great poets walk through eternity eneveloped and disguised. It is a difficult question to determine how far they were conscious of the distinction which must have subsisted in their minds between their own creeds and that of the people...Milton's poetry contains within itself a philosophical refutation of that system of which, by a strange and natural antithesis, it has been a chief popular support. Nothing can exceed the energy and magnificence of the character of Satan as expressed in *Paradise Lost*. It is a mistake to suppose that he could ever have been intended for the popular personification of evil. Implacable hate, patient cunning, and a sleepless refinement of device to inflict the extremest anguish on an enemy, these things are evil; and, though venial in a slave, are not to be forgiven in a tyrant; although redeemed by much that ennobles his defeat in one subdued, are marked by all that dishonours his conquest in the victor. Milton's Devil as a moral being is as far superior to his God, as one who perseveres in some purpose which he has conceived to be excellent in spite of adversity and torture, is to one who in the cold security of undoubted triumph inflicts the most horrible revenge upon his enemy, not from any mistaken notion of inducing him to repent of a perseverance in enmity, but with the alleged design of exasperating him to deserve new torments. Milton has so far violated the popular creed (if this shall be judged to be a violation) as to have alleged no superiority of moral virtue to his god over his devil. And this bold neglect of a direct moral purpose is the most decisive proof of the supremacy of Milton's genius.

[See also Shelley's *Prometheus unbound* and preface.]

WILLIAM BLAKE from *The marriage of Heaven and Hell c.* 1793

Those who restrain desire, do so because theirs is weak enough to be restrained; and the restrainer or reason usurps its place and governs the unwilling.

And being restrained, it by degrees becomes passive, till it is only the shadow of desire.

The history of this is written in *Paradise Lost*, and the governor or Reason is called Messiah.

And the original archangel, or possessor of the command of the heavenly host, is called the Devil or Satan, and his children are called Sin and Death.

But in the Book of *Job*, Milton's Messiah is called Satan.

For this history has been adopted by both parties.

It indeed appeared to Reason as if Desire was cast out; but the Devil's account is, that the Messiah fell, and formed a heaven of what he stole from the abyss... The reason Milton wrote in fetters when he wrote of angels and God, and at liberty when of devils and hell, is because he was a true poet and of the Devil's party without knowing it.

Other examples of the romantic Satan: Charles Baudelaire *Les litanies de Satan c.* 1840; Roy Campbell *The flaming terrapin* 1924; D. H. Lawrence *Lucifer* (two versions) and *Old archangels* in *More pansies.*

Satan in other arts

For portraits of Satan see Goya; Bruegel *Dulle Griet* ('Mad Meg'); and some of the illustrators of *PL*, especially Medina (Book 1), Hayman (11 with Sin), Hogarth, Fuseli, Blake, and Doré. From these you will see the trend in concepts of the Evil One through the series monster...tyrant...madman...rake...resentful son ...Byronic hero (not necessarily in that order). He is more usually an actual part of hell – e.g. the sculpted Last Judgements on the cathedrals of Autun (12c) and Bourges (13c), the illuminations in *Les très riches heures du Duc de Berry* (Chantilly 15c).

Music: listen to Rimsky-Korsakov *Night on the bare* (or *bald*) *mountain* 1908, adapted from Mussorgsky's *St John's night on the bare mountain* 1867, about a witches' sabbath; S. R. Leslie's musique concrète *Death of Satan* MC 1001.

Psychology of the satanic

W. H. AUDEN from *The enchafèd flood or the romantic iconography of the sea* 1951 [Taking off from Kiekegaard on despair and the demonic, and talking about Claggart, the devil figure in Melville's *Billy Budd*] ...paradoxes are raised by the demonic, the religious passion in reverse. For the demonic must be moved solely by pride, just as the religious must be moved solely by faith and love. Absolute pride cannot be manifested aesthetically because it tolerates no weakness except itself which thinks of itself as absolute strength.... The Devil, therefore, cannot himself be lustful, gluttonous, avaricious, envious, slothful, or angry, for his pride will not allow him to be anything less than proud. He can only pretend in disguise to be any of these without actually feeling them; he can only 'act' them. His acts must appear to be arbitrary and quite motiveless. No accurate aesthetic portrayal, therefore, is possible; Iago has to be given some motive, yet if the motive is convincing, he ceases to be demonic.

You might follow up 'the religious passion in reverse' in Angel Clare's role in Hardy's novel *Tess of the D'Urbervilles*: see David Lodge *Language of fiction* (1966) II iv. See also J. C. Flugel *Man, morals and society: a psychoanalytical study* 1945 Pelican, especially ch. 11 on 'The need for punishment'; and Ernest Jones *On the nightmare* 1931.

Other telescope passages at IV 42, III 590, V 261, *PR* IV 41, *Vac Ex* 71. See a good history of science and consider why the sciences that *poets* have made use of since *c.* 1400 seem to go in the series astrology, alchemy, mineralogy; astronomy; biology; physics. Or is that the series of dominant sciences? The interpretation of the Galileo metaphor at 288 is very complicated. Satan overdoes Achilles, via their shields; this should not mean that Satan is more heroic than Achilles, but that Achilles' heroism is ultimately irrelevant – 'easily outdone by spirits reprobate' like human engineering (696). In any case, Homer's Achilles was a lovelorn sulk as well as a great warrior; and in Shakespeare's *Troilus* Thersites calls him 'a valiant ignorance' III iii 320 and 'idol of idiot-worshippers' V i. Yet Satan's superiority is as it were achieved with Galileo's help, i.e. the help of human science. Does this mean that science is Satanic, like the technology of Pandemonium? If so, Milton has damned Galileo whom he claimed to have visited; and joined the Inquisition who had put Galileo under house-arrest. Or are we meant to read the passage as Galileo's intelligence transcending Satan's heroics, as well as Achilles', so that the simile damns with praise too loud?

Fallen angels

We often take a specialized view of poetry: it is a means of communication demanding rare sensitivity at both ends; it exists for its own being – 'A poem should not mean but be'. 17c poets would not have agreed. We may therefore think it legitimate to follow Milton when, in this section, especially the parade of gods, he writes as an anthropologist, geographer, historian – an historian of culture, religion and science.

On angels generally, see *PL: introduction* in this series, and the introduction to Satan above. The theoretical issue is extensive. An angel is clearly not a man, but higher, for Jesus 'made himself a little lower than the angels' at the incarnation. An angel must therefore be some sort of god; but doesn't that mean polytheism?

By studying the good and evil angels of any period you can get some idea of what were then thought to be the extreme virtues and vices; or, what were thought to be the opposites or corruptions of any good.

The finest sustained piece of prose on good angels is chapter 5 of D. H. Lawrence's *Rainbow*.

Parade of idols

Ancient middle-eastern religion is a complicated subject, largely in the hands of archaeologists and theologians, not accustomed to explaining things to other people. The sort of treatment that's needed is hinted at in a feature on the New English Bible by Marcelle Bernstein in the London *Observer* colour supplement 15 March 1970. It contains pictures of Ashtoreth and a baal. The best work for pulling all these fields together is W. G. de Burgh *The legacy of the ancient world*, rev. ed. 1947.

ST PAUL *Epistle to the Romans*
...the invisible things of him from the creation of the world are clearly seen, being understood by the things that are made, even his eternal power and Godhead; so that they are without excuse: because that, when they knew God, they glorified him not as God, neither were thankful; but became vain in their imaginations, and their foolish hearts were darkened. Professing themselves to be wise, they became fools, and changed the glory of the uncorruptible God into an image made like to corruptible man, and to birds, and fourfooted beasts, and creeping things. Wherefore God also gave them to uncleanness through the lusts of their own hearts, to dishonour their own bodies between themselves: who changed the truth of God into a lie, and worshipped and served the creature more than the Creator, who is blessed for ever. Amen.   i 14–25

History of Israel

Start with Solomon's succession to David *I Kings* i, and a decent Bible commentary. Here is a rough chronology with special reference to this section of *PL*:

BC	Israel and Judah	Elsewhere
8000		Cultivation begins
2234		Astronomical observations begin to be recorded at Babylon
2000	Abraham, Isaac, Esau and Jacob	
1700	Joseph in Egypt	
1300	Exodus from Egypt. Moses, Aaron. Wandering in wilderness. Settlement in Canaan: Joshua	Rameses II of Egypt
1040	King Saul	
1020	King David. Kingdom consolidated	
980	King Solomon. Oriental despotism; worship centralized at temple in Jerusalem	
937	Separation into Israel (Northern kingdom) and Judah (S)	Homeric writings in Greek?
876	King Ahab of Israel	

BC	Israel and Judah	Elsewhere
842	Israel falling under power of Assyria.	Hesiod *Theogony?*
736	King Ahaz of Judah. Idolatry. Judah falling to Assyria	
640	King Josiah of Judah: reformation.	
607	Assyrian empire wanes; Babylonian waxes. Jeremiah	Nebuchadnezzar of Babylon
586	Babylonians sack Jerusalem and take people of Judah captive	Persian empire supreme
458	Some return to Jerusalem under Ezra	Golden age of Athens
332	Jews submit to Alexander the Great	
168	Jerusalem sacked, temple profaned; Israel under Rome	Rome supreme

Conflicting values

The phrase 'Memphian chivalry' 307 is one of a series of sneers at the fallen angels in terms of an outmoded knighthood; cf. 534 737, IV 769, VI 168, XII 210, *PR* III 342. There is a parallel series in terms of oriental barbarism, e.g. I 348 377 717, II 1, X 457. But opinions differ on how sincerely M rejected these worldly glamours. Here is Bentley arguing that I 580 cannot be genuine:

Milton indeed in his prose works tells us, That in his youth he was a great lover and reader of romances; but surely he had more judgement in his old age than to clog and sully his poem with such romantic trash as even then when he wrote was obsolete and forgot. To stuff in here a heap of barbarous words, without any ornament or poetical colouring, serving only to make his own argument, which he takes from the Scripture, to be supposed equally fabulous, would be such pedantry, such a silly boast of useless reading, as I will not charge him with.

MALCOLM M. ROSS *Milton's royalism: a study of the conflict of symbol and idea in the poems* Ithaca N.Y. 1943

The vanity and evil of earthly monarchies are suggested in poetic terms indistinguishable from those which suggest the splendor of Heaven. By inserting signposts, by telling us when to feel 'This is vain' and 'This is glorious', Milton seeks to keep his distinctions clear...That he fails is evident, and that he is conscious of the dilemma in which he finds himself is equally evident.

One might expect that if knights, warriors and conquerors are the evil 'Plagues of men' (XI 698), the warriors of hell would be evil indeed, and their trappings the very symbol of evil. Such is not the case. The allusion to British fable (I 580) is meant to conjure up positive visions of grandeur.

Belial...is not a knight. He is not valorous. He is contemptible...But if his counsel had been accepted, Adam would not have been visited by evil. On the other hand, Beelzebub, who urged war against God through the seduction of Man, *is* regal...

J. B. BROADBENT *Some graver subject: an essay on PL* 1960

When these passages are read, one by one, as they come in the poem, they are fit: swift rhythm flashes the remote references across an already distant screen...If we pause at the oases we find they are more: they are like Prufrock's mermaids and the glimmers of beauty in *The Waste Land*, ironic. Milton's yearning is not irrelevantly for the damsels and Mulciber and so on *per se*, but for their loss, the corruption of love into Syrian sexiness, the fall of human expertise into Hell's technological aggrandisement...We may suspect that in both parading and condemning all that vainglory [chivalry etc.] Milton was trying to have his cake and eat it. The reader who from the first line recognised *Paradise Lost* as an epic, but one bearing a peculiar relationship to all previous epics, would expect sooner or later a display of armed might simply as a *tour de force*...The subject of the passage is not so much the devils as Homer and Virgil, Tasso and Spenser: their work is taken up, outdone, and consigned to Hell.

A. J. A. WALDOCK *PL and its critics* 1947

In any work of imaginative literature at all it is the demonstration, by the very nature of the case, that has the higher validity: an allegation can possess no comparable authority. Of course they should agree; but if they do not then the demonstration must carry the day.

Barbarians

The name comes from *ba-ba* (cf. modern American *yawp*): what foreign languages sounded like in Greek ears. This raises the question of how far barbarism (and barbarity?) is something we attribute to aliens just because they are alien; and how far there actually are successive waves of barbarism breaking civilization down, and then perhaps reinvigorating it? Milton's barbarians are the ancestors of all NW European peoples. The issue lies below what we feel about 'immigrants'.

The Victoria and Albert Museum, London, contains an introduction to 'barbaric' art; and see a book which deals with a specific culture, e.g. Henry Bradley *The Goths: from the earliest times to the end of the Gothic dominion in Spain* 1888 Story of the Nations.

MILTON *Academic exercise* (Prolusion) v composed while an undergraduate trans. and ed. Phyllis Tillyard Cambridge 1932

The Romans, masters of the world in ancient time, attained the highest summit of power, which neither the vastness of Assyria nor the martial prowess of Macedon could reach, and to which the majesty of kings in time to come will never be able to exalt itself...However this may be [Jupiter] did not allow them to enjoy this privilege without earning it, but only granted it to them after constant wars and prolonged toil... And so they were compelled to live a life of abstinence and hardship, and to find the new pleasures of peace always cut short by war's alarms and the clash of arms around them. In addition to this, they were under the necessity of providing garrisons...and of sending nearly all their young men either to distant wars or to their colonies...Moreover the victories they gained were not always bloodless; on the contrary, they often suffered grievous disasters...Lastly, the Goths and Vandals under their king Alaric, and the Huns and Pannonians under their leaders Attila and Bleda passed in a torrent over the whole of Italy, cruelly plundered the abounding riches of the empire, the accumulated spoils of so many wars, overwhelmed in shameful flight the Romans, who were but now the lords of mankind, and captured the city, captured Rome herself, by the mere terror of their name.

EDWARD GIBBON *The decline and fall of the Roman Empire* 1776–87
 ch. 38 'General observations on the fall of the Roman Empire in the west'

The Romans were ignorant of the extent of their danger and the number of their enemies. Beyond the Rhine and Danube the northern countries of Europe and Asia were filled with innumerable tribes of hunters and shepherds, poor, voracious, and turbulent; bold in arms, and impatient to ravish the fruits of industry. The barbarian world was agitated by the rapid impulse of war; and the peace of Gaul or Italy was shaken by the distant revolutions of China. The Huns, who fled before a victorious enemy, directed their march towards the West; and the torrent was swelled by the gradual accession of captives and allies. The flying tribes who yielded to the Huns assumed in *their* turn the spirit of conquest; the endless column of barbarians pressed on the Roman empire with accumulated weight...Such formidable emigrations no longer issue from the North...The reign of independent barbarism is now contracted to a narrow span...Yet this apparent security should not tempt us to forget that new enemies and unknown dangers may *possibly* arise from some obscure people, scarcely visible in the map of the world. The Arabs or Saracens, who spread their conquests from India to Spain, had languished in poverty and contempt till Mahomet breathed into those savage bodies the soul of enthusiasm.

Charlemagne, chivalry, crusades

Charlemagne (AD 768–841) is a useful bridge-figure: himself a Frank, i.e. of barbarian stock, he was an ally of the Pope and defeated the Arabs in Spain. It was as he withdrew into France again through the Pyrenees that Roland (Ariosto's Orlando) was treacherously trapped at Roncesvalles 'and all his peerage fell' near Fuentarabia. To warn Charlemagne, Roland with all his men dead around him blew his horn so loud that the birds fell out of the sky and his heart burst. For the history see Jacques Boussard *The civilisation of Charlemagne* trans. F. Partridge 1968 World University Library. It may be that a study of history can ease the problem of values in this area of the poem – heroism versus

Christianity etc. As soon as the new barbarian inhabitants of Europe stabilized they started to attack the east as crusaders.

Geography of Israel

Public communications have caused us to give up that part of geography which consists in being able to find your way about. Unfortunately that means that we can't find our way about in imagination either. Milton's first readers were mentally well acquainted with the geography of the middle east. Maps were included in some Bibles; there were the records of the great explorers (Hakluyt, Purchas, Heylyn etc.); and there were contemporary accounts of Palestine, e.g. *A relation of a journey begun AD 1610: four books, containing a description of the Turkish empire, of Egypt, of the Holy Land, of the remote parts of Italy and islands adjoining* 1615 by George Sandys, devout paraphraser of psalms and Bible stories into doggerel; and *A Pisgah-sight of Palestine and the confines thereof, with the history of the Old and New Testaments acted thereon* 1650 by Thomas Fuller, preacher and biographer. We have nothing to compare with these. The maps in the backs of Bibles particularly are useless. The only consolation is that the area is very small: Jerusalem–Cairo=London–Paris. Still, an opportunity offers for doing some geography on the middle east which would begin with such questions as why it seems to have been the cradle of cities and philosophies.

Hell

Described at 1 60 180 192–350 531 670, 11 87 213 570–628, IV 20 75, X 410. What are hell's characteristic features? and how do we distinguish them from the *images* used to describe it, or the sensations associated with it? Can we reconcile hell as a place of punishment with hell as a rallying-place for the devils, hell as an internal state, and as a condition of human being ('L'enfer, c'est les autres' – Sartre)? These problems were familiar to the 17th century. Here are a few of their reflections, some other examples, and a list of works about hell.

17th-century hells

MILTON *Doctrine and discipline of divorce* 1643
To banish for ever into a local hell, whether in air or in the centre, or in that uttermost and bottomless gulf of chaos, deeper from holy bliss than the world's diameter multiplied; they [classical poets and philosophers] thought not a punishing so proper and proportionate for God to inflict, as to punish sin with sin.

BENJAMIN WHICHCOTE (1609–83) sermon
The wicked and profane...think that they were out of danger, if God would forbear a positive infliction; and that hell is only an incommodious place, that God by his power throws them into. This is the grand mistake. Hell is not only a positive infliction...the fuel of Tophet burning is the guiltiness of man's conscience, malignity, and a naughty disposition against goodness and holiness; and God's withdrawing because the person is incapable of his communication. Sin is an act of violence in itself: the sinner doth force himself, and stirs up strife within himself; and in a sinner there is that *within* which doth reluctate, and condemn him in the inward court of his own conscience.

JOHN SMITH (1618–52) *A Christian's conflicts and conquests*
Would wicked men dwell a little more at home, and descend into the bottom of their own hearts, they should soon find hell opening her mouth wide upon them, and those secret fires of inward fury and displeasure breaking out upon them which might fully inform them of the estate of true misery, as being a short anticipation of it. But in this life wicked men for the most part elude their own misery for a time, and seek to avoid the dreadful sentence of their own consciences, by a tergiversation and flying from themselves into a converse with other things.

SIR THOMAS BROWNE *Religio medici* 1643
Men commonly set forth the torments of hell by fire, and the extremity of corporal afflictions, and describe hell in the same method as Mahomet doth heaven...men speak too popularly who place it in those flaming mountains, which to grosser apprehensions represent hell. The heart of man is the place devils dwell in: I feel sometimes a hell within myself; Lucifer keeps his court in my breast, Legion is revived in me.

THOMAS DEKKER from *Dekker his dream: in which, being rapt with a poetical enthusiasm, the great volumes of Heaven and Hell to him were opened, in which he read many wonderful things* 1620
[At the final conflagration of the world, Dekker flees to hell]

...The way was quickly found: paths numberless	*Facilis*
(Beaten with feet which thither fast did press)	*descensus Averni*
Lay trodden bare; but not one path returning	*Vestigia nulla*
Was ever seen from this dark house of mourning.	*retrorsum*

This flaming kingdom had one ferryman,
And he one boat; he rows through Acheron,
Styx, and Cocytus, rivers that in Hell
Spread all the country o'er; fogs still dwell
Stinking and thick upon them, and there grows
Upon their banks, in wild disordered rows,
The poplar, white and black, with blasted yew,
The deadly poppy, cypress, gall, and rue
(Emblems of graves, tombs, funerals, and biers);
And on the boughs no other bird appears
But schriches, owls, and ravens, and the shrill throats
Of whistlers: death still listening to their notes.

.   .   .   .

I hollo'ed to the ferryman (methought)
And with a stretched voice cried, A boat! a boat!
He came at first call, and when near he drew,
That of his face and form I had full view,
My blood congealed to ice with a cold fear
To see a shape so horribly appear:
His eyes flashed fire, grizzled and shagged his hair
(Snarled all in feltlocks); terror and despair
Lay in his wrinkled cheeks; his voice was hoarse
And grumbling; he looked ghastlier than a corpse.

*This description of
the ugly ferryman is
but an argument how
terrible the appearance
of death is unto us, at
our last voyage,
which we take in
departing from the
world . . .*

Other hells

WILLIAM BLAKE from *Vala, or the four Zoas*: Night the sixth 1797
Not so closed kept the Prince of Light now darkened, wandering among
The ruined spirits, once his children and the children of Luvah:
For Urizen beheld the terrors of the abyss, wandering among
The horrid shapes and sights of torment in burning dungeons and in
Fetters of red hot iron; some with crowns of serpents and some
With monsters girding round their bosoms; some lying on beds of sulphur,
On racks and wheels; he beheld women marching o'er burning wastes
Of sand in bands of hundreds and of fifties and of thousands, strucken
  with
Lightnings which blazed after them upon their shoulders in their march
In successive volleys with loud thunders: swift flew the King of Light
Over the burning deserts. Then, the deserts passed, involved in clouds
Of smoke with myriads moping in the stifling vapours, swift
Flew the king, though flagged his powers, labouring till over rocks
And mountains faint weary he wandered where multitudes were shut
Up in the solid mountains and in rocks which heaved with their torments.
Then came he among fiery cities and castles built of burning steel.
Then he beheld the forms of tigers and of lions, dishumanized men.
Many in serpents and in worms, stretched out enormous length
Over the sullen mould and slimy tracks, obstruct his way
Drawn out from deep to deep, woven by ribbed
And scalèd monsters or armed in iron shell, or shell of brass
Or gold: a glittering torment shining and hissing in eternal pain;
Some, columns of fire or of water, sometimes stretched out in heighth,
Sometimes in length, sometimes englobing, wandering in vain seeking
  for ease.
His voice to them was but an inarticulate thunder, for their ears
Were heavy and dull, and their eyes and nostrils closed up.
Oft he stood by a howling victim questioning in words
Soothing or furious; no one answered; everyone wrapped up
In his own sorrow howled regardless of his words, nor voice
Of sweet response could he obtain, though oft assayed with tears.
He knew they were his children ruined in his ruined world.

.   .   .   .

When he had passed these southern terrors he approached the east,
Void, pathless, beaten with iron sleet, and eternal hail and rain.
No form was there, no living thing, and yet his way lay through
This dismal world; he stood a while and looked back over his former

Terrific voyage, hills and vales of torment and despair!
Sighing, and weeping a fresh tear, then turning round, he threw
Himself into the dismal void; falling he fell and fell,
Whirling in unresistible revolutions down and down
In the horrid bottomless vacuity, falling, falling, falling
Into the eastern vacuity, the empty world of Luvah...

JAMES JOYCE from *Ulysses* 1922 [Here is the opening of the underworld
   section. This hell is the slum of Dublin where the hero, Leopold Bloom,
   and his son Stephen Daedalus, end the day in a brothel.]
The Mabbot street entrance of nighttown, before which stretches an
uncobbled tramsiding set with skeleton tracks, red and green will-o'-the-
wisps and danger signals. Rows of flimsy houses with gaping doors. Rare
lamps with faint rainbow fans. Round Rabaiotti's halted ice gondola
stunted men and women squabble. They grab wafers between which are
wedged lumps of coal and copper snow. Sucking, they scatter slowly.
Children. The swancomb of the gondola, highreared, forges on through
the murk, white and blue under a lighthouse. Whistles call and answer.

THE CALLS

Wait, my love, and I'll be with you.

THE ANSWERS

Round behind the stable.
   (A deafmute idiot with goggle eyes, his shapeless mouth dribbling,
jerks past, shaken in Saint Vitus' dance. A chain of children's hands
imprison him.)...

Other arts

Wagner *Gotterdämmerung* (Twilight of the gods)=4th part of
opera *The Nibelungs' ring* 1876. Stravinsky *Rite of spring* 1913
ballet.

Many *Last Judgements* and *Temptations of St Antony*. *Hell* (right
wing) and *Last Judgement* (centrepiece) of triptych attributed to
Hieronymous Bosch (*d.* 1516) in Vienna Academy of Fine Arts;
and his *Hell* (inner right wing of triptych *The garden of earthly
delights*) Prado, Madrid. Rodin *The gates of hell* (multifarious
colossal sculpture) and *Fall of the angels*. There are 16th-century
Paduan bronze models of the mountain of hell in the Victoria and
Albert Museum A62– and A63–1953; classical details such as
Sisyphus included.

Pandemonium

See the story of the Tower of Babel in *Genesis* x, Bruegel's
paintings of it, and Gozzoli's *City of Babylon* (repr. in Berenson's

Italian paintings of the renaissance); Bosch's hells; the engravings of Piranesi. The fine illustration to the episode by John Martin resembles Albert Speer's design for a Nazi chancellery (*TLS* 16 October 1969). Milton probably had the Pantheon in mind, or St Peter's – one pagan, one catholic, both Roman. Gibbon was to describe the temple of Serapis (*PL* 1 720) from the other side.

Metamorphosis. Change had a bad name in Christian literature partly because of Ovid's *Metamorphoses*: a number of the changes Ovid tells of there were effected by Zeus so that he could seduce girls; or by girls trying to escape. There are two ends to the matter. The anthropological end is that when a myth tells of a god changing into a swan or a girl into a tree we are listening to harmonies played on the relationship between – and hence the identities of – god, bird, human, tree. The personal–social end is that when we say 'You've changed!' we mean something different from 'How you've grown!' It has to do with change being into the unexpected, the wrong, like that in Kafka's story *Metamorphosis*.

Technological guilt. See the story of Prometheus, in all its ramifications, in Graves's version (Penguin *Greek myths*); Freud *Civilisation and its discontents* 1939; Claude Lévi-Strauss *Le cru et le cuit* (*The raw and the cooked*) Paris 1964 trans. 1970.

The ancient metaphor of mining as incestuous rape of mother earth that Milton uses at 687 might spring from either, or both, of these histories: (a) technology may not be so purposeful as it looks; it may be the expression of unconscious sexual drives, ultimately towards the mother, which cannot be gratified and so take the form of aggression, power, control (something like this is obvious in the sexual symbolism of cars); (b) the invention of cultivation and herding *c.* 8000 BC did start to ruin the earth; the ruin was only hastened by the subsequent extraction of metals, building of cities, irrigation (say 4000 BC).

Appendix to Book II

Debate in Pandemonium

Issues for debate

The debate raises some fundamental and ethical questions. It is inadvisable to think about more than one at a time.

By what merit does anyone deserve to be a ruler or leader? (II 5, 18). Supposing merit and election disagree?

Mammon mocks the courtliness and reverence of heaven as servile (242, cf. VI 168); yet the peers of hell imitate heaven every way they can, and worship Satan on their faces (477): is all ceremony false? It is defended by C. S. Lewis in *Preface to PL* 1942 ch. xi and Yeats *Prayer for my daughter*. Can we avoid the devils' emulation of the very thing we despise?

Milton contrasts hard and strenuous liberty with servile pomp, ignoble ease (227 255, *SA* 271): what forms might these opposites take? is the contrast a valid one? surely there is something to be said for quietly offering the tyrant a flower, and something to be said against violent resistance? In any case, does the strenuous exercise of liberty – eternal vigilance – actually do any good?

What may be said for the doctrine of 'labour and endurance' 262? It looks like a doctrine of puritanism or the Pilgrim Fathers; why does M put it in the mouth of the devil?

Beelzebub is a pillar of state 302. These sturdy figures are to be found in all corridors of power. Is it better for people to do the work that suits their temperament and physique even when it means we are mostly governed by one type?

Round 395 and elsewhere the devils deal in chance and fate. Milton implies that these are inferior to more definite moral principles such as right and wrong, and to divine powers. Is this so?

At 482 M allows that the fallen angels may act virtuously – with courage, for instance, or loyalty – just as evil men may. This raises the issue of humanism (based on virtue) versus religion (which has a spiritual or supernatural element). What is that extra element precisely? And what is it that makes for evil in some men who are brave or clever or in other ways virtuous? In short, what do we mean by good?

See *Milton: introductions* and the section on Miltonic concepts in *PL: introduction* in this series. M's other passages of political poetry are mostly linked to the characters and concerns of this debate, e.g.:

Monarchy and tyranny	*War*	*Wealth*
PL v 350 577 769, xi 381 656, the fallen world's equivalent of Pandemonium. xii 63 tyranny. x 410 Satan's return to hell. *PR* ii 432 and iv 109 Christ's rejections of earthly kingship.	*PL* v–vi war in heaven. xi 552 war in the fallen world. *PR* iii 386 Christ's rejection of war.	*PL* i 678; *PR* ii 432 Christ's rejection of riches, cf. *Comus* 760.

One of the difficulties in Milton's position was that he objected to kingship, yet had to accept Cromwell as a dictator; and that he objected to Satan's command over hell, yet had to use some of the traditional oriental imagery of kingship for God. Here are two passages from his prose on kingship; see also Malcolm M. Ross *Milton's royalism: the conflict of symbol and idea in the poetry.*

From *Defensio pro populo anglicano* 1651
I confess many eminent and famous men have extolled monarchy; but it has always been upon this supposition, that the prince was a very excellent person, and one that of all others deserved best to reign; without which supposition, no form of government can be so prone to tyranny as monarchy is. And whereas you resemble a monarchy to the government of the world by one Divine Being, I pray answer me, whether you think that any other can deserve to be invested with a power here on earth that shall resemble his power that governs the world, except such a person as does infinitely excel all other men, and both for wisdom and goodness in some measure resemble the Deity? And such a person, in my opinion, none can be but the Son of God himself. And whereas you make a kingdom to be a kind of family, and make a comparison betwixt a prince and the master of a family, observe how lame the parallel is: for a master of a family begot part of his household – at least he feeds all those that are of his house, and upon that account deserves to have the government; but the reason holds not in the case of a prince; nay, it is quite contrary.

From *Defensio secunda* 1654
Nothing in the world is more pleasing to God, more agreeable to reason, more politically just, or most generally useful, than that supreme power should be vested in the best and wisest of men. Such, O Cromwell, all acknowledge you to be; such are the services which you have rendered, as the leader of our councils, the general of our armies, and the father of

your country. For this is the tender appellation by which all the good among us salute you from the very soul. Other names you neither have nor could endure; and you deservedly reject that pomp of title which attracts the gaze and admiration of the multitude. For what is a title but a certain definite mode of dignity? But actions such as yours surpass, not only the bounds of admiration, but our titles; and, like the points of the pyramids, which are lost in the clouds, they soar above the possibilities of titular commendation.

But since, though it be not fit, it may be expedient, that the highest pitch of virtue should be circumscribed within the bounds of some human appellation, you endured to receive, for the public good, a title most like to that of the father of your country; not to exalt, but rather to bring you nearer to the level of ordinary men. The title of king was unworthy the transcendent majesty of your character. For if you had been captivated by a name over which, as a private man, you had so completely triumphed and crumbled into dust, you would have been doing the same thing as if, after having subdued some idolatrous nation by the help of the true God, you should afterwards fall down and worship the gods which you had vanquished.

Rhetoric, sophistry; good and bad language

Milton attacks Belial's oratory at 112 and there is a continuous implicit satire on rhetoric; at IX 670 Satan's tempting is compared to Greek and Roman eloquence; at *PR* IV 240 he tempts Christ with it and is rejected:

> Their orators thou then extoll'st, as those
> The top of eloquence, statists indeed,
> And lovers of their country, as may seem;
> But herein to our prophets far beneath,
> As men divinely taught, and better teaching
> The solid rules of civil government
> In their majestic unaffected style
> Than all the oratory of Greece and Rome.   353

Yet God speaks rhetorically in III, and Milton himself has been blamed for writing with more noise than sense:

He exhibits a feeling *for* words rather than a capacity for feeling *through* words...the words...seem...to be occupied with valuing themselves rather than with doing anything.

F. R. LEAVIS *Revaluation* 1936

Milton's own oratorical style has indeed associated him with an 'establishment' felt to be remote, pompous, unintelligible, insulating himself against the raw with big Latin words learned at fee-paying schools. Is there *any* case for rhetoric? The classic discussion is by Plato in the *Gorgias c.* 405 BC. Gorgias was one of the sophists, or teachers of oratory, who emerged in Athens in the

5th and 4th centuries BC. They emerged because it was essential in that small, highly participatory democracy for a citizen to know how to put his point and sway a debate. Is sophistry the price of participation? See also Aristophanes' comedy *The clouds*.

F. R. LEAVIS from *Revaluation* 1936
So complete, and so mechanically habitual, is Milton's departure from the English order, structure and accentuation that he often produces passages that have to be read through several times before one can see how they go, though the Miltonic mind has nothing to offer that could justify obscurity – no obscurity was intended: it is merely that Milton has forgotten the English language. There is, however, a much more important point to be made: it is that, cultivating so complete and systematic a callousness to the intrinsic nature of English, Milton forfeits all possibility of subtle or delicate life in his verse.

Satan's speech to Sin at 817 is a good place to start making a list of unnecessary obscurities and dislocations. What sort of badness is it in say 846 901 1033? Do we find necessary obscurities in 11? Consider 362–78, which was set by one of the public examining boards in England in 1963. One of the questions was 'Distinguish between "The puny habitants", "his darling Sons", "their frail originals"'. It seems unlikely that the examiner knew how much he was asking. Editors have disagreed for 300 years about whether Adam and Eve are cursing the frailty of their original natures, or we are cursing their frailty as our originals – all sorts of interpretations are possible because Milton is fusing the meanings in a characteristic way; and there was a textual emendation in the 2nd edition. If you do plump for a single answer, you get caught by the pun in *puny*.

CHRISTOPHER RICKS in *Milton's grand style*
Hume's gloss ran: 'The weak infirm Possessors, the late made Inmates of this new World: *Puisne*, born since, created long since us, Angelick Beings boasting Eternity.' And Newton developed the point: 'It is possible that the author by *puny* might mean no more than weak or little; but yet if we reflect how frequently he uses words in their proper and primary signification, it seems probable that he might include likewise the sense of the French (from when it is deriv'd) *puis né*, born since, created long after us.' Again it is only a matter of making more explicit the double meaning which Hume and Newton so admirably fasten on. That Man was 'born since' the fallen angels is precisely the great reason why they hate him...

On the whole we are likely to agree with Leavis that such language 'calls pervasively for a kind of attention, compels an attitude towards itself, that is incompatible with sharp, concrete realization; just as it would be, in the mind of the poet, incompatible with an interest in sensuous particularity'. Compare, for instance, Milton's presentation of death with almost any in Shakespeare: Claudio's speech in *Measure for measure* III i, which includes traditional details of hell –

> To bathe in fiery floods, or to reside
> In thrilling regions of thick-ribbèd ice;
> To be imprisoned in the viewless winds,
> And blown with restless violence round about
> This pendent world

– or 'So, now prosperity begins to mellow and drop into the rotten mouth of death' (*Richard III* IV iv), or Herbert's poem *Death*. We see that Milton's epic character is less sharply personified than the metaphors of Shakespeare and Herbert. Ultimately perhaps it is a mistake to cast experiential forces like death, evil, grace, onto an epic screen. See Broadbent 'Milton's mortal voice and his omnific word' in *Approaches to PL* ed. Patrides 1968.

What does Milton's method offer then? The best thing is to accept his abstractions, as large labels; then reflect on our own experience of them. It is we who have to provide the examples, the particularity, the experience. We all rule vain empires. We may be able to read the 'darling sons' and 'frail originals', according to our own experience, in terms of an elegy for lost youth, or breach between those frail originals or parents, or between them and us. It is of no importance to learn that 'hatching vain empires' is a sneer at Moloch or even that it is a parody of the Holy Ghost. There may be some point, though, in reflecting on the complex of ideas hatching–generating–conceiving–concept.

Obviously we could go on from here either towards larger topics or smaller ones. On the larger side, we have such questions as what is hellish about Milton's hell (or sinful about his Sin)? Why do most hells share certain characteristics such as fire, volcanoes, huge buildings, monsters, ice? Is there anything in Satan that we find unredeemable, entirely alien? If we talk about a condition such as pride, courage, despair in terms of theology, and then of psychiatry, are we still talking about the same thing? Of smaller, more technical questions we notice (to take that exam-set passage as an example) words which recur in *PL* – *frail* associated with *fall*, *fraud*, *false* etc. Does this have an effect beyond mere noise? What effect on the blank verse do the more rhyming sorts of repetition have – *surpass–upraise–curse–bliss–worth*? Some of Milton's epithets seem significant – *puny*, *darling*; what about such qualifiers as *whole* and *headlong*? There are several words in that passage which might be called religious – *repenting* for example; how do Milton's religious words sort with other kinds such as political and military?

MILTON from *Of reformation in England and the causes that have hitherto hindered it* 1641 [An example of one of Milton's prose styles which might be related to the verse style he uses for *PL* I–II]

O sir, I do now feel myself enwrapped on the sudden into those mazes and labyrinths of dreadful and hideous thoughts, that which way I turn to get out, or which way to end, I know not, unless I turn mine eyes and with your help lift up my hands to that eternal and propitious throne where nothing is readier than grace and refuge to the distresses of mortal suppliants; and it were a shame to leave these serious thoughts less piously than the heathen were wont to conclude their graver discourses.

Thou, therefore, that sittest in light and glory unapproachable, Parent of angels and men! Next, thee I implore, omnipotent King, Redeemer of that lost remnant whose nature thou didst assume, ineffable and everlasting Love! And thou, the third subsistence of divine infinitude, illumining Spirit, the joy and solace of created things! One tripersonal Godhead! Look upon this thy poor and almost spent and expiring church, leave her not thus a prey to these importunate wolves, that wait and think long till they devour thy tender flock; these wild boars that have broke into thy vineyard and left the print of their polluting hoofs on the souls of thy servants. O let them not bring about their damned designs, that stand now at the entrance of the bottomless pit, expecting the watchword to open and let out those dreadful locusts and scorpions to reinvolve us in that pitchy cloud of infernal darkness, where we shall never more see the sun of thy truth again, never hope for the cheerful dawn, never more hear the bird of morning sing. Be moved with pity at the afflicted state of this our shaken monarchy, that now lies labouring under her throes, and struggling against the grudges of more dreaded calamities...

Then, amidst the hymns and hallelujahs of saints, some one may perhaps be heard offering at high strains in new and lofty measure to sing and celebrate thy divine mercies and marvellous judgments in this land throughout all ages; whereby this great and warlike nation, instructed and inured to the fervent and continual practice of truth and righteousness, and casting far from her the rags of her whole vices, may press on hard to that high and happy emulation to be found the soberest, wisest, and most Christian people at that day, when thou, the eternal and shortly expected King, shalt open the clouds to judge the several kingdoms of the world, and distributing national honours and rewards to religious and just commonwealths, shalt put an end to all earthly tyrannies, proclaiming thy universal and mild monarchy through heaven and earth; where they undoubtedly, that by their labours, counsels, and prayers, have been earnest for the common good of religion and their country, shall receive above the inferior orders of the blessed, the regal addition of principalities, legions, and thrones into their glorious titles, and in supereminence of beatific vision, progressing the dateless and irrevoluble circle of eternity, shall clasp inseparable hands with joy and bliss, in overmeasure for ever.

Sin and Death

The introduction indicates relevant mythology. The scene at hellgate was one of the most popular for illustrators: see especially Hayman (reproduced in Broadbent *Some graver subject*), Blake and Fuseli; for further details see *Milton: introductions* and *PL: introduction* in this series, and Marcia R. Pointon *Milton and English art* 1970.

C. G. JUNG *Psychology of the unconscious: a study of the transformations and symbolisms of the libido: a contribution to the history of thought* trans. Beatrice Hinkle 1919 ch. 4

In consciousness we are attached by all sacred bonds to the mother; in the dream she pursues us as a terrible animal. The Sphinx, mythologically considered, is actually a fear animal, which reveals distinct traits of a mother derivative. In the Oedipus legend the Sphinx is sent by Hera, who hates Thebes on account of the birth of Bacchus; because Oedipus conquers the Sphinx, which is nothing but fear of the mother, he must marry Jocasta, his mother, for the throne and the hand of the widowed queen of Thebes belonged to him who freed the land from the plague of the Sphinx. The genealogy of the Sphinx is rich in allusions to the problem touched upon here. She is a daughter of Echnida, a mixed being: a beautiful maiden above, a hideous serpent below. This double picture corresponds to the picture of the mother; above, the human, lovely and attractive half; below, the horrible animal half, converted into a fear animal through the incest prohibition. Echnida is derived from the All-mother, the mother Earth, Gaea, who, with Tartaros, the personified underworld (the place of horrors), brought her forth. Echnida herself is the mother of all terrors, of the Chimaera, Scylla, Gorgo, of the horrible Cerberus, of the Nemean Lion, and of the eagle who devoured the liver of Prometheus; besides this she gave birth to a number of dragons. One of her sons is Orthrus, the dog of the montrous Geryon, who was killed by Hercules. With this dog, her son, Echnida, in incestuous intercourse, produced the Sphinx. These materials will suffice to characterise that amount of libido which led to the Sphinx symbol.

NORMAN O. BROWN from *Life against death: the psychoanalytical meaning of history* 1959 ch. 9 'Death and childhood'

The purely biological act of birth which not only destines the organism to death but is in itself the death of a foetus as well as the birth of a baby, is also a biological separation from the mother conferring biological individuality on the child. The prototype of psychic traumas, the experience of wanting but not being able to find the mother, is an experience of psychic separation, and its anxiety is, in Freud's own words, 'the anxiety of separation from the protecting mother' [*The ego and the id* 1927]. And the climactic psychic trauma, castration anxiety, is, according to Freud, also a fear of separation from the mother, or rather a fear of losing the instrument for reuniting with a mother-substitute in the act of copulation. Furthermore all these separations are experienced as a threat of death: again in Freud's own words, what the ego fears in anxiety 'is in the nature of an overthrow or extinction'...Anxiety is a response to experiences of separateness, individuality, and death...It is because the child loves the mother so much that it feels separation from the mother as death. As a result, birth and death, which at the biological level are experienced once only, are at the human psychic level experienced constantly: the child can say with St Paul, 'I die daily'.

One effect of the incapacity to accept separation, individuality, and death is to erotize death – to activate a morbid wish to die, a wish to regress to the prenatal state before life (and separation) began, to the mother's womb...

The following texts, in conjunction with that from *James* quoted in the introduction, locate death in Christian doctrine. They show that the difficult doctrine of atonement is based on a structure in which Christ also is a god of death – King, killed, embalmed, buried, he harrowed hell, and rose again (the seasonal return); but is still celebrated in terms of death by the eating of his flesh and blood:

Wherefore, as by one man sin entered into the world, and death by sin; and so death passed upon all men, for that all have sinned...as by one man's disobedience many were made sinners, so by the obedience of one shall many be made righteous. *Romans* v

For as in Adam all die, even so in Christ shall all be made alive.

I Corinthians xv 22

Some 17th-century poems about death: George Herbert *Death*. John Donne *Holy sonnets* (most of them); *Anniversaries*: see his funeral sermons on James I and on Lady Magdalen Herbert (or Danvers); and extracts 124–34 in *Selected passages* from his sermons ed. L. P. Smith 1919. Richard Lovelace *La bella bona-roba*. Henry Vaughan *The charnel-house*.

VIRGIL's account of Cerberus in Tartarus: *Aeneid* VI 412 [Charon ferries Aeneas and his guide the Cumean Sibyl across the Styx]
                              simul accipit alveo
          ingentem Aeneam. gemuit sub pondere cumba
          sutilis et multam accepit rimosa paludem.
          tandem trans fluvium incolumis vatemque virumque
          informi limo glaucaque exponit in ulva.
              Cerberus haec ingens latratu regna trifauci
          personat, adverso recubans immanis in antro.
          cui vates, horrere videns iam colla colubris,
          melle soporatam et medicatis frugibus offam
          obicit. ille fame rabida tria guttura pandens
          corripit obiectam, atque immania terga resolvit
          fusus humi totoque ingens extenditur antro.

                         and took on board
          Aeneas's vast body, under which, groaning,
          The hulk sank lower sucking in the marsh through caulkless
              seams.

146

On ghastly muck of mud and weed priestess and hero
Over the channel land unharmed at last.
   Here the air howls with baying from the three throats
Of the Head, its monstrous body kennelled in a cave.
The heckles of its three necks rose bristling with snakes;
Rabid, famished, its three mouths gaped – and caught
Before it fell the drugged bait the Sibyl flung:
Colossally relaxing, sinking to the earth,
Over the floor of the whole cavern its frame collapses.

The finest musical evocation of hellgate is Monteverdi's in Act III of *Orfeo*.

Chaos

The other descriptions of chaos in *PL* are:

   III 705 Uriel briefly describes creation.

   VII 192 the Son rides into chaos to create the world.

    X 235 Sin and Death fly into chaos to bridge it from hell to the world (anti-creation).

    X 648 The angels alter the solar system after the fall, bringing something of chaos into it, stylistically.

   XI 466 The lazar-house, also a stylistic parallel.

See *PL: introduction* in this series for the Babylonian myth of how the divine hero Marduk slew Tiamat, the she-monster, and made the world out of her carcase. Tiamat is the origin of the Biblical notion of chaos, and of leviathan and the dragon of the deep. In other words, that which is unformed (shapeless, primordial, pre-creation) gets pushed into the role of that which is wrong (unnatural, monstrous, evil, anti-creation) within the created universe. The questions to ask are, What do we actually feel about the primordial? Do we want to go back to it, or to some created stage? Why does the complex chaos–wrong have so much to do with what is liquid, and with snakes? Do these conflations affect the art of *PL*? Some of the following excerpts may serve as comment on these questions, and on M's definition of chaos as both womb and grave (911).

17th-century meditations on death faced its physical events; and so provide evidence for the identity in myth of death and chaos. Here is JEREMY TAYLOR (see *The golden grove* – selections ed. L. P. Smith 1930):

I have read of a fair young German gentleman, who living, often refused to be pictured, but put off the importunity of his friends' desire by giving way that after a few days' burial they might send a painter to his vault, and if they saw cause for it, draw the image of his death unto the life. They did so, and found his face half eaten, and his midriff and backbone full of serpents; and so he stands pictured among his armed ancestors.

Holy dying 1651

So are the desires and weak arts of man, with little aids and assistance of care and physic we strive to support our decaying bodies and to put off the evil day; but quickly that day will come, and then neither angels nor men can rescue us from our graves; but the roof sinks down upon the walls, and the walls descend to the foundation; and the beauty of the face, and the dishonours of the belly, the discerning head and the servile feet, the thinking heart and the working hand, the eyes and the guts together shall be crushed into the confusion of a heap, and dwell with creatures of an equivocal production, with worms and serpents, and sons and daughters of our own bones, in a house of dirt and darkness.

Funeral sermon for Lady Carberry 1650

MIRCEA ELIADE from *The myth of the eternal return* [*Le Mythe de l'éternel rétour: archétypes et répétition* Paris 1949 rev. 1965] trans. W. R. Trask, New York 1954

We must not forget that, apart from its possible role in the rites and myths of heroic initiation, the dragon, in many other traditions...is given a cosmological symbolism: it symbolises the involution, the pre-formal modality, of the universe, the undivided 'One' of pre-Creation (cf. Ananda K. Coomaraswany, *The Darker Side of Dawn*, Washington, 1935...). This is why snakes and dragons are nearly everywhere identified with the 'masters of the ground', with the autochthons against whom the newcomers, the 'conquerors', those who are to form (i.e. create) the occupied territories, must fight.

Ch. 1, sect. 'Myths and history', note 70

The lines about Lucretius in the introduction are from Tennyson's poem (1864) on how his nymphomaniac wife gave him an aphrodisiac which drove him mad so he killed himself. Lucretius's atomic theory derives from the Greek philosophers Democritus and Epicurus. Here is his description of chaos in *De rerum natura*:

At that time the sun's bright disc was not to be seen here, soaring aloft and lavishing its light, nor the stars that crowd the far-flung firmament, nor sea nor sky nor earth nor air nor anything in the likeness of the things we know – nothing but a hurricane raging in a newly congregated mass of atoms of every sort. From their disharmony sprang conflict, which maintained a turmoil in their interspaces, courses, unions, thrusts, impacts, collisions and motions, because owing to their diversity of shape and pattern they could not all remain in the combinations in which they found themselves or mutually reconcile their motions. From this medley they started to sort themselves out, like combining with like, and to rough out the main features of a world composed of distinct parts: they began, in fact, to separate the heights of heaven from the earth, to single out the sea as a receptacle for water detached from the mass and to set apart the fires of pure and isolated ether.

VI 416 trans. R. E. Latham, Penguin 1951

Lucretius (whom Milton had read) was a sceptic:

As for Cerberus and the Furies and the pitchy darkness and the jaws of hell belching abominable fumes, these are not and cannot be anywhere at all. But life is darkened by the fear of retribution for our misdeeds, a fear enormous in proportion to their enormity, and by the penalties imposed for crime – imprisonment and ghastly precipitation from Tarpeia's Crag, the lash, the block, the rack, the boiling pitch, the firebrand and the branding iron. Even though these horrors are not physically present, yet the conscience-ridden mind in terrified anticipation torments itself with its own goads and whips. It does not see what term there can be to its suffering nor where its punishment can have an end. It is afraid that death may serve merely to intensify pain. So at length the life of misguided mortals becomes a hell on earth.   Book III

ALEXANDER POPE from *The Dunciad* (i.e. the epic of the dunce) 1726
                In eldest time, ere mortals writ or read,
        Ere Pallas issued from the Thunderer's head,
        Dulness o'er all possessed her ancient right,
        Daughter of Chaos and eternal Night;
        Fate in their dotage this fair idiot gave,
        Gross as her sire, and as her mother grave;
        Laborious, heavy, busy, bold, and blind,
        She ruled, in native anarchy, the mind.
        Still her old empire to restore she tries
        For, born a goddess, Dulness never dies.

    .   .   .   .

        Here she beholds the Chaos dark and deep
        Where nameless somethings in their causes sleep,
        Till genial Jacob, or a warm third day,
        Call forth each mass – a poem or a play;
        How hints, like spawn, scarce quick, in embryo lie,
        How newborn nonsense first is taught to cry,
        Maggots half-formed in rhyme exactly meet
        And learn to crawl upon poetic feet.

    .   .   .   .

        Swearing and supperless the hero sat,
        Blasphemed his gods, the dice, and damned his fate;
        Then gnawed his pen, then dashed it on the ground,
        Sinking from thought to thought, a vast profound!
        Plunged for his sense, but found no bottom there,
        Yet wrote and floundered on in mere despair.
        Round him much embryo, much abortion lay,
        Much future ode and abdicated play;
        Nonsense precipitate like running lead
        That slipped through cracks and zigzags of the head;
        All that on Folly Frenzy could beget,
        Fruits of dull Heat, and sooterkins of Wit...
                                            Book I

149